CLASSROOM STRATEGIES THAT WORK

CLASSROOM STRATEGIES THAT WORK

An Elementary Teacher's Guide to Process Writing

Ruth Nathan
Frances Temple
Kathleen Juntunen
Charles Temple

Heinemann
Portsmouth, New Hampshire

HEINEMANN EDUCATIONAL BOOKS, INC.
361 Hanover Street   Portsmouth, NH   03801-3959
Offices and agents throughout the world

The publishers and the authors wish to thank the children, teachers, and parents whose words and writings are quoted here for permission to reproduce them, and to the following for permission to quote from previously published works:

Section 1 of this book is based on portions of *The Beginnings of Writing*, Second Edition, by Charles Temple, Ruth Nathan, Nancy Burris, and Frances Temple, copyright © 1988, 1982 by Allyn and Bacon, Inc. Reprinted by permission of Allyn and Bacon, Inc.
Figure 1–31, "The Qualities of Good Writing" by Donald M. Murray, is reprinted by permission of the author.

Every effort has been made to contact the copyright holders and the children and their parents for permission to reprint borrowed material. We regret any oversights that may have occurred and would be happy to rectify them in future printings of this work.

LIBRARY OF CONGRESS
Library of Congress Cataloging-in-Publication Data

Classroom strategies that work : an elementary teacher's guide to
    process writing / Ruth Nathan . . . [et al.].
        p.   cm.
    Includes bibliographies and index.
    ISBN 0-435-08479-8
    1. English language—Composition and exercises—Study and
teaching (Elementary)   2. Language arts (Elementary)—Correlation
with content subjects.   I. Nathan, Ruth G.
LB1576.C5638 1989
372.6'23—dc19   88-17602
                                                                      CIP

Designed by Marie McAdam.
Cover by Max-Karl Winkler.
Printed in the United States of America.
10   9   8   7   6   5   4   3

"Do you think your writing is worth doing—as an end in itself?"

"Oh, yes."

"You are sure?"

"Very sure."

"That must be very pleasant."

"It is," I said. "It is the one altogether pleasant thing about it."

Ernest Hemingway
Green Hills of Africa

Contents

Preface
Ruth Nathan

If one believes that there are teachers in this world who would ignore a bird flying through their classroom window, then perhaps there is some truth in the old adage "Good teachers are born, not made." Except for such blatant blindness, however, the saying doesn't hold much water for us, the authors of your new book. We certainly believe that we've been made, and that we continue to change each and every day we work with youngsters.

Of course teachers are made! We've been made by our own personal histories: how we were taught to whittle, build a go-cart, tie our shoes, write Grandma, set the table, read a book, ride a bike, or climb a tree. We've been made by the teachers we've encountered in school ourselves. And as teachers we continue to be made by the children we teach, as we listen and learn what we must do to engage and inspire our newcomers.

Eight years ago, without our even knowing it, *Classroom Strategies That Work* was being written. Charles, Frances, and I sat on the Temple living room floor in Victoria, Texas, finishing our first collaborative text, *The Beginnings of Writing*. (Allyn and Bacon published that book back in 1982, with Nancy Burris as a co-author.) It was to be a textbook on the writing aspect of emerging literacy. At that time, however, we were already wishing that we could go beyond second grade. Frances and I were working in elementary classrooms and had more to explore. And Charlie was teaching teachers, searching, with them, for ways to keep older elementary students writing creatively. Reluctantly, we closed the books on *The Beginnings*, promising ourselves to get back together in the near future.

The second edition of *Beginnings* provided us with that opportunity. With Frances and me in classrooms much or all of the week, a new chapter had emerged detailing how to get process-writing classrooms going in entire districts. Talk of a new book began in earnest.

Allyn and Bacon has been kind enough to let Heinemann begin this book with that new chapter on process writing. We thank Allyn and Bacon for their generosity. Though slightly embellished, Section 1 of *Classroom Strategies That Work* is very similar to Chapter 11 of the second edition of *The Beginnings of Writing*. We've gone on in this book, however, to sketch in some focused lessons and to share our approaches to writing across the curriculum. We've also added a new member to our writing team, Kathy Juntunen, who's been working with me for the past two years in Birmingham, Michigan.

Yes. Teachers are made. If there weren't some truth to that, you wouldn't be reading this book in the first place, and we wouldn't find ourselves delighted and inspired by the books and articles Donald Graves, Lucy Calkins, Donald Murray, Tom Romano, Toby Fulwiler, Christopher Thais, Ron Cramer, Eileen Tway, Nancie Atwell, Jane Hansen, and many other scholars continually write. We wouldn't drink up *Language Arts* each month, or that powerful and eminently helpful new journal, *The New Advocate*. We're all made, daily, continually growing into our roles as teachers of the language arts. Whether birds fly through our windows or not, children walk through our doors each day, and that, combined with our mutual sharing, is all any of us really needs.

Acknowledgments

Ruth Nathan wishes to thank the following people for their gracious and continuous giving:

her family—Larry, Julie, Amy, and Emily—who continually support her writing by saying everything is splendid, just splendid —even eighth drafts;

the children from the Birmingham and Walled Lake public schools, who expect that fabulous ideas are not around the corner, but in their pencils;

Sylvia Whitmer, principal of Oakley Park Elementary, and Bud Davies, assistant superintendent of Walled Lake public schools, for their brilliant appraisal of situations and possibilities;

fellow writing consultants Kathy Juntunen, Heidi Wilkins, and Julie Janosz, for their ears and feedback;

her Peninsula Writer friends;

her good friends, Michael Steinberg, the Temples, and Keith Stanovich and Shirley Neitzel, for their informed criticism;

and lastly, her mother, Doris Greenbaum, and her oldest friend, Viola Wilkins, who, like her husband and children, encourage, encourage, encourage.

Kathleen Juntunen is indebted to Reta Grey, Nancy Austin, Carol Cote, and Alice Trocke, all talented Birmingham, Michigan, public school teachers, who allowed her the privilege of working with their students; and to the supportive Pierce School parents and students, who willingly participated in the Authors' Night evaluation: Deb Wagoner, John Thomas, Diane Tallinger, Jeff Stringfield, Ryan Sarver, Alan and Mary Ann Linck, Ben Holman, Jeremiah and Colleen Farrell, Barbara Ann Cromar, and Vanessa Callaghan.

Thanks also go to students Norishige Abe and Brandi Blaisdell for their illustrations, and Owen Blank, Becky Lincoln, and Andrea Schachterle for allowing use of their writing.

Very special thanks go to Ruth Nathan, who gave unstintingly of her time and talent as a conference partner in the writing of this book.

Frances Temple thanks the children, parents, and teachers at Children's Hours School for their spacious ideas and cheerful participation, Meredith Moodie for the opportunity to develop new ways of teaching, and Debbie D'Angelo for poems and levity.

Charles Temple doffs his hat to his students, family, Ruth, and Ma Bell.

PRINCIPLES FOR TEACHING THE WRITING PROCESS

Charles Temple

As a teacher and writer, and sometimes as a teacher of writing, I have over the years learned a handful of hard-won lessons about my craft. Each of these lessons at one time had the flash of discovery about it. But, of course, many other teachers have had similar insights: the other three authors of this book, though their experiences as teachers and writers differ from mine as much as they overlap, have reached similar conclusions about teaching writing and place like value on them. These insights unite us professionally, and without them we couldn't have written this book. They became, in fact, our guiding principles, forming the foundation for our interaction with one another.

Here is my list of lessons, and a brief description of how I came to learn each one.

1. *Students write best about topics that matter to them, to audiences that are interested in their ideas.* Many of us have seen children, who at other times labor to fill in single letters in dull workbook pages, suddenly take off and soar when allowed to write about their own experiences and their favorite things for an audience they care about, especially when teachers relax the emphasis on convention. Look at the three first-grade examples in Figure I–1.

I first learned of the power of the self-chosen topic and an audience of one's peers in the 1960s, teaching English in a high school exclusively for black students. They and I caught a sense of the power of the written word as they exchanged letters with students at the white high school we were going to integrate the next year, using paper and pen to say who they were and what they hoped for and feared about this fast approaching end to three hundred years of social separation.

I learned that lesson all over again when I was teaching writing in a commuter college for older students. A man who could string barbed wire and help bring reluctant calves into the world;

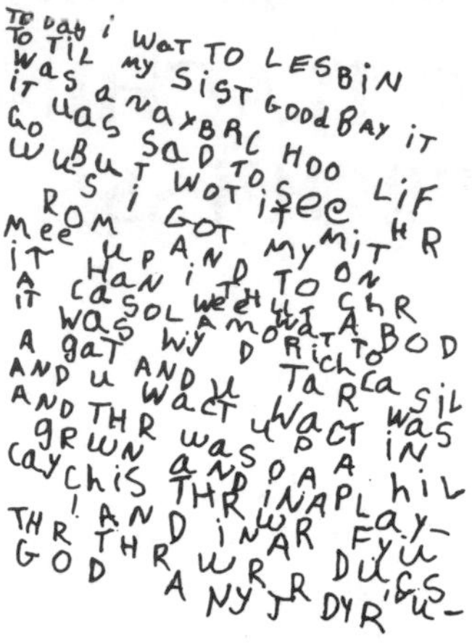

Today I went to Lisbon to tell my sister good-
bye. It was Annabrook who left. It was sad to see
her go, but what it meant was I got my own
room, and to cheer me up I thought about it.
Then we went to a castle, a Moorish castle. It
was windy. There was a gate and you walked in
and you walked up a hill and there in a garden
there was a playground, and in a few cages there
were three goats, and in another a few ducks and
another deer.

(a)

(b)

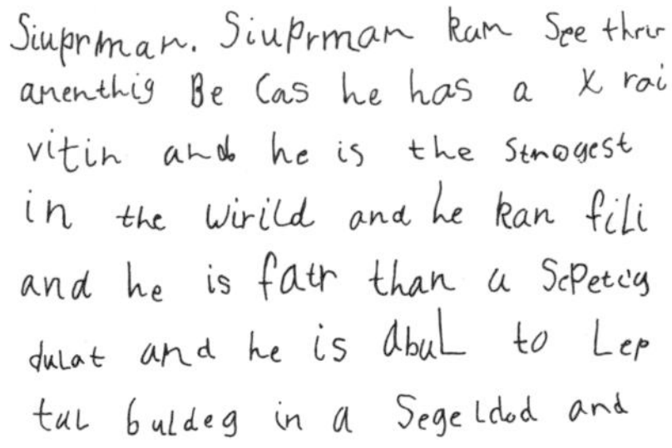

(c)

**FIGURE I–1 Three First-Grade Examples of Writing. (a) Tyler. (b) JoBeth.
(c) Ian.**

a woman who could nurse the sick and bury the dead; a woman who had eaten fried chicken with Elvis Presley on the back of his secondhand Cadillac when he was an unknown; a woman who had divorced a cheating husband; a man who had found religious faith with a force so sudden he thought he'd been struck by lightning—any of these people would rather have handled a live rattlesnake than hand in a paper. That is, until they realized that they could write about their experiences and fascinate readers with them, that they could have their classmates and their writing teacher reading about the events of their lives and begging for more. Whether used by adults or by children, writing to communicate with others has an appeal and a force that makes writing its own best teacher.

2. *Given the chance to serve as an audience for each other, a class-room full of students can teach each other to write better than a single teacher can.* The year was 1954. A second-grade classmate of mine hit on the idea of drawing cartoons during art time. He divided a large sheet of that cream-colored, pulpy paper into a dozen boxes and filled each one with pencil-drawn figures, complete with words in balloons attached to each character. The idea spread like a grassfire; art time became composing time, and the amount of writing each one of us churned out that year increased fivefold.

In the past five years, I have had many opportunities to observe a child read a draft of a paper to his classmates and listen quietly as first the others praised it and then asked questions, aired their confusion over certain points, and ultimately encouraged the writer to fill in more details.

In the same Texan commuter college I mentioned earlier, I divided my students into groups and had them take turns reading their papers to each other. They read them one at a time to me, too, and I tried to show them how a person could comment helpfully on what another had written. After hearing the group's comments, or mine, the students rewrote their papers and tried them out on an audience a second time. The surprising thing is that at the end of the term, the students demonstrated that they had learned more about writing—not only about having something to say and finding a voice to say it in but also about paragraphing, sentence structure, and the like—than the students in other sections of the same writing course taught through the lecture and drill method.

— 3. *We write best when we have models around us to show us how to write. Model* here has a double sense. In one we mean demonstrations of the act of composing; in another we mean models of written products. Donald Graves has come up with a metaphor for the first kind of modeling. Writing, he says, is a studio craft. Teaching writing is best approached the same way as teaching someone to throw pots: you don't simply show the finished product and exhort the student to go and do likewise; you demonstrate right before the eyes of the class the way the hands gouge, push, pull, and raise smooth walls from a spinning lump of clay.

In the Children's Hours School the primary-grade children have a part of every day reserved for what is called writing workshop time, a forty-minute period during which the children begin to write new topics or continue writing on ones they began on previous days. This period always begins the same way: everybody writes, including the teacher. When the teacher says, "I need quiet in here," she is not voicing some abstract management principle; she is demonstrating firsthand a genuine need to concentrate. When later she talks of her difficulty in finding a beginning for a piece, the children come to know that even grown-ups have to confront problems in putting thoughts on paper. But what is more, the teacher can identify these problems, give them names, and invite children to discuss and find solutions to them.

The other sense of the word *modeling* is this: Children need examples of literary forms to use as points of departure for their own creations. Nobody creates from nothing; indeed, the more familiar we become with literature the more we see how much authors have influenced each other. Reading and discussing literature with children gives them access to language, forms, and devices they can use in their own writing. Take the example presented as Figure I–2 from Tyler, age seven, who had just read and enjoyed Russel Hoban's "Egg Thoughts" before writing her own poem.

4. *Even though we try to put our students in the driver's seat, nurturing their own initiative as writers as fully as possible, there are times when it is simply more economical to teach limited points directly.* Direct teaching is a delicate matter, however. We have learned, as I said before, that having students write what they want is better than using up their writing time with explanations and exercises. We find we teach best when, in addition to devoting daily blocks of time for the students to write works of their own choosing and sharing these works with others, we also set aside occasional blocks of time for direct teaching of limited issues when we see the need for them.

In a first-grade classroom, it is common to find that children who are composing freely don't always remember to leave spaces

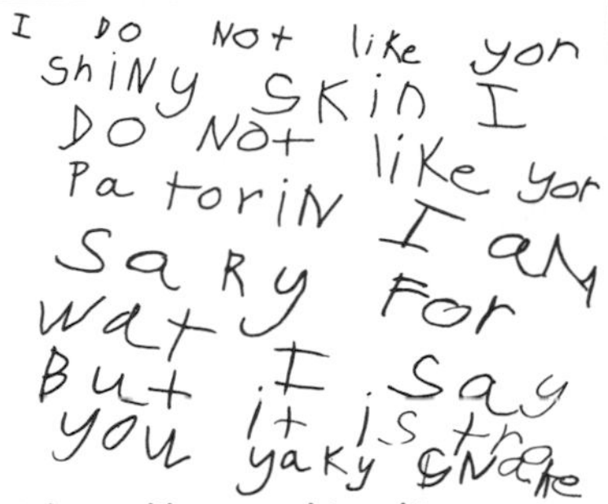

I do not like your shiny skin,
I do not like your pattern.
I am sorry for what I say
But it is true, you yucky snake.

FIGURE I–2 Tyler, Age 7

between words. With the permission of one young writer, we made a transparency of one of his drafts that had this problem and projected the paper for all to see. After discussing the message of his paper, and finding things to praise about it, we asked if members of the class could help us find the individual words. When they did, we wrote each sentence over again, this time leaving a space between the words. When next the children were writing, we reminded them to leave spaces between the words in just the way we had demonstrated on the overhead. Later, perhaps years later, we will use the method of direct teaching to show children strategies for writing good beginnings to their pieces, how to add information, how to organize their ideas, how to punctuate dialog, and so on.

5. Finally, and in many ways for me this is the payoff: *When we write, we often tell ourselves things we didn't know we knew.* This lesson is pressing itself upon me with special force here in Spain, where I am teaching a seminar for a group of American college students. A scrap of a conversation overheard on the street becomes raw material for further learning the moment it is written down. A visit to a cathedral—written first as dry notes and later expanded with personal reflections—takes us spiraling up from description to reaction to insight, from thinking about the cathedral to thinking about how and why we think these thoughts about the cathedral, so that we arrive at a new awareness of our ideas of beauty, dignity, and grace; of our feelings about religion, about power, and about culture.

Writing can encourage younger children to reflect, too. Sarah was in the second grade when her class made a field trip to a nearby cemetery to make headstone rubbings. The cemetery was very old; some of the graves of soldiers in the American Revolution had American flags on them. The children were curious about the flags, and later, on the way home, there was a discussion of soldiering. Afterwards, Sarah wrote the following piece:

At the Graveyard

by Sarah

At the graveyard there are lots of people that fought in the Civil War. They have flags by their gravestones. It makes me feel sad but still they fought to keep us alive.

But still I feel sorry.

In short, writing is not so much a subject as an intellectual force, and we can learn to use it with any number of subjects to get far more out of our studies.

That covers the five principles I wanted to share about teaching and learning to write. Here they are again:

1. Students write best about topics that matter to them, to audiences who are interested in their ideas.
2. Given the chance to serve as an audience for each other, a classroom full of students can more effectively teach each other to write than a single teacher can.
3. Students write best when they have *models* around to show them how to write (by models we mean both written products and people who are writing).
4. Sometimes it is more effective to teach certain limited points about writing directly.
5. By writing, people can often tell themselves things they didn't know they knew. Writing gives people a means to move from observation to reaction to reflection. Writing is thus a powerful tool for learning in all subjects.

In this book we present practical classroom strategies based on these principles.

We approach this topic in three sections. The first, on setting up and managing a classroom for teaching writing, includes how to help children choose topics for writing, how to confer with them to help them develop their ideas, ways of developing the responding skills of groups of children, ways of teaching children to edit their work, and options for publishing what children write. Also included in this section are suggestions for the very first steps a teacher takes to introduce process writing, through more and more refined teaching strategies to carry the teacher and the group further along.

The second section expands on an idea we introduced above: that it is occasionally useful to teach a limited lesson directly on some aspect of writing. In this section we argue for the idea of *focused lessons*, and share several that have proved successful with children of different ages.

The third section shows how opportunities to write can be found across the curriculum; how writing can be used to deepen learning in all subjects; and, to the extent that writing and reading are inseparable, how literature contributes to the same end.

SETTING UP A WRITING PROGRAM
Ruth Nathan

Introduction

In the introduction to this book we set out the principles that organize our collective approach to teaching writing—letting the students choose their own topics, using peers as an audience, teaching and using writing to learn about other things. In this section we begin by describing the activities inherent in the writing process itself—what people do when they write. Then we plunge into the main work of the chapter: spelling out detailed procedures for setting up and managing a writing program.

A Description of the Writing Process

There is obvious good reason for understanding the writing process if we are going to teach it. But one particular advantage lies in the discovery that writing is not just one activity but several, and how we, as teachers, can show students how to perform these several acts in coordination.

Donald Murray, a Pulitzer Prize–winning writer who is a teacher of writing, has come up with perhaps the clearest description of the interlocking activities that make up the writing process (Murray, 1980). In Murray's model, writing is a *process of continuous thinking, experimenting, and reviewing.* The activity of writing a paper develops in three stages: rehearsing, drafting, and revising.

Rehearsing is the stage in which writers assemble the raw materials of what they are going to say. They collect observations and think of what is interesting about them. They find connections between ideas they had not seen before. Rehearsing takes the raw stuff of experience and begins to find language for it, or takes hazy but attractive ideas and begins to focus them around a point. Implicit in the idea of rehearsing is thinking about "who cares?"—thinking about the way a topic could be focused and extended to be of interest to others.

When we teach children to write, we often take an action that a mature writer carries out privately in her mind and get the children to practice it outwardly and publicly; we assume that they will learn to perform it inwardly and privately later on (Vygotsky, 1980). Thus, in teaching children to rehearse, we often involve them in interesting experiences that they may wish to talk about and write about. We ask them to talk about their topic and decide what is most important or most interesting about it, or to trade roles with another child and get *him* to ask questions about what he thinks is most interesting about the first child's topic. We may ask older children to brainstorm, to make a preliminary list of details about a topic, or to web, that is, to draw graphic connections between ideas. In sum, methods for rehearsal are intended to bring out into the open a wide range of particular ideas and details that a writer can subsequently use in her deliberate writing. We will discuss such methods in detail later on.

Drafting is the second stage in the process of writing. The term is chosen because this sort of writing is tentative: when we speak of a first draft or a second draft we imply that a piece is undergoing change, and that other drafts may follow. If there is one thing that experienced writers know that novices don't, it is how to take it easy on themselves while drafting—not to worry about spelling, not to be critical of their ideas, but to let their thoughts flow onto the page as freely as possible. In approaching the writing easily they are really showing more of a commitment to it: they know that if it is good, they will work on it more than once, that they may take it through several drafts to make it right.

Writers often surprise themselves with their ideas when they draft. Peter Elbow believes that the physical act of writing somehow loosens up writers' thoughts and lets them flow out more easily than they do when writers deliberately plan—that is, when they try to think directly about what they are going to say (Elbow, 1973). Murray (1980) describes drafting as a time when writers put down their ideas on paper so that they can see what they know about a topic.

Lucy Calkins (1986) has a nice phrase for teaching children to draft: "Make it messy to make it clear." We teach children how to cut drafts apart and tape them back together again in a better order, to mark out unwanted sections, to use carets, arrows, and other proofreader's marks to show changes that should be made between one draft and another.

Revising is the final stage, although we should remember that revision can lead to further rehearsal and further drafts. The writer examines her piece and clarifies for herself what the writing should say. When necessary, the writer prunes words or adds them, all in an effort to make the meaning that is in the piece speak more clearly. Sometimes revising is a matter of patching up phrases or sentences in order to make them smoother or clearer. Sometimes, however, the writer discovers whole new possibilities that should be developed in the work. In the latter event, revision can mean changes to larger parts of a work, and sometimes to the whole work. In Murray's words (1980), "The writing stands apart from the writer, and the writer interacts with it, first to find out what it has to say, and then to help the writing say it more clearly and gracefully."

Along the lines of making private acts public, we teach children to revise by teaching them to question their own and others' works and by subjecting their works to comments of an audience. We hope they will eventually internalize this audience so they are able to imagine them when they reach the stage of revising—but not before, lest the writers become too inhibited to write. We develop these ideas at much greater length later on.

Now let's put the writing process to work. What follows is a discussion of a writing program that has proven successful for us and for the teachers with whom we work. The program is sensitive to the composing process Murray describes and to the important areas of the writing teacher's responsibility: atmosphere and response.

A Writing Program: Grades One Through Six

In the remainder of Section 1 we will discuss a general system for implementing a writing program for first through sixth grades—a system that is sensitive to the writing process Murray describes (1980) and to the classroom characteristics that support writing growth. The discussion will be divided into eight sections:

1. an overview of a process-writing classroom;
2. an outline of what to do the first day;
3. a typical day;
4. suggestions for setting up a writing classroom in general, and writing folders in particular;
5. the dynamics of moving a promising draft along;
6. conferencing techniques;
7. publishing possibilities;
8. suggestions for evaluation.

We have found this system to work well for us over the years, but we assume that our techniques will be modified by anyone who chooses to use them. We have not found it easy, by any means, to set up and sustain process-writing classrooms, but the rewards continue to make the effort worthwhile. We reflect with pleasure on the honest industry we have seen each day in children who are writers, the sound of pencils scratching furiously across page after page of text, the earnest voices of children talking to one another about their evolving drafts, the pride we see in children's faces as they share their finished products, and the heightened, almost collegial curiosity our young authors show about the adult authors who write the stories they read and love.

AN OVERVIEW OF A PROCESS-WRITING CLASSROOM

In process-writing classrooms we attempt to create an atmosphere where even a professional writer would feel at home. Here children choose their own topics and write for people that matter:

themselves, their classmates, their friends in the school community (pieces are shared between classrooms), their teacher, their parents and siblings, as well as the literary community at large (work is submitted for publication).

You will see boxes that hold writing folders; trays for works in progress; jars of pencils, crayons, and colored markers; shelves of published books; an author's chair; and bulletin boards, which sometimes celebrate a published author, but just as often celebrate a member of the class. Large round tables are placed well apart for group conferences, and small places are created (spaces under tables, for example) where pairs of children can collaborate in peace.

Though a part of each writing period is quiet, perhaps fifteen minutes, a good portion—twenty minutes, or so—is not. Like professional writers, children are encouraged to talk to others about their drafts. They talk to their teachers and their classmates. They ask for an ear, first to attend to meaning and later to attend to grammar and style. They ask for an eye, first to attend to spelling and later to attend to mechanics.

Writing is a cooperative effort between teachers and children in these classrooms. It is joyful, noncompetitive, and nourishing, while at the same time highly demanding. Children write at length, they revise, and they edit, but in an atmosphere of acceptance and *respect*. This milieu has been set up and maintained with several purposes in mind, but perhaps the major purpose has been to prevent loathing of the whole process later on, as Peter nearly did (see Figure 1–1).

FIGURE 1–1 Peter, Grade 1

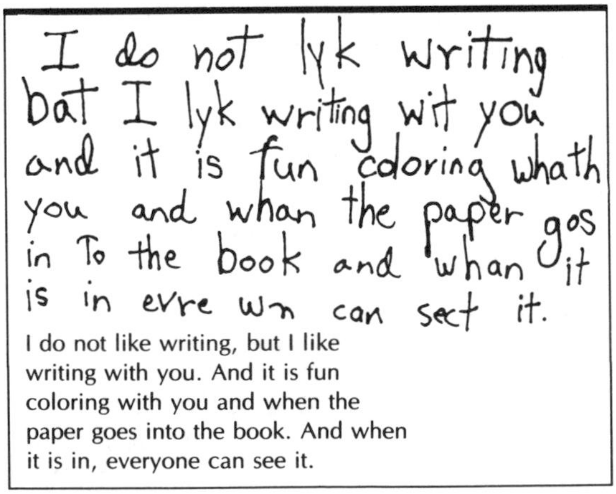
I do not lyk writing
bat I lyk writing wit you
and it is fun coloring whath
you and whan the paper gos
in To the book and whan it
is in evre wn can sect it.

I do not like writing, but I like writing with you. And it is fun coloring with you and when the paper goes into the book. And when it is in, everyone can see it.

AN OUTLINE OF WHAT TO DO
THE FIRST DAY

According to Donald Graves (1983), the tone is set in process-writing classrooms by what the teacher *does*, not by what the teacher *says*. We agree. First you will have to show children how you go about making your own topic choices; an overhead projector is helpful here. We tend to choose topics that conjure up lots of memories or ones that would make us feel good in the writing. Yesterday I worked on a topic list with one of my fourth-grade classes. My list embraced eight close-to-home possibilities: Nana (my grandmother); windsurfing on Glen Lake; making chicken soup; K-Mart shopping; Marilyn (a best friend from childhood); my cat, Sammy; listening to my daughter, Julie, practice; and birds playing by a stoplight on a road close to my home.

I wrote these topics on the overhead while I slowly chatted about each one with the children. Here's an excerpt from my topic-generating demonstration.

I think I must have a book in my head about *my grandmother*—she just died a few months ago. When I was your age I used to go to her apartment on weekends—so different from my house, so much like a grandma's place—you know, glass animals on wooden shelves, lace doilies covering her overstuffed chairs, cookies. A grandma's place. I could write about that.

Windsurfing. Yes, I've just learned how. Lots of funny times, like the day a stranger called from shore, "Hey lady, would you tell my boys, dinner's on?" Dinner's on? I thought. Those boys were out there in the middle of the lake, and I was just a beginner! Boy, I was scared, but I was much too embarrassed to tell that man I probably couldn't get there. I might write about that. . . .

Marilyn. She was my best buddy when I was a kid. We did everything together: We built a cemetery in her back yard. We had a playhouse for years, and spent whole weekends together making poisons and potions —in order to put trances on people we didn't like and to stir up dimples and freckles—you know. Once we ran away—a stupid idea. I remember asking Marilyn, who had phoned to ask me if I would, "Why do you want to do a thing like that?" I can hear her screaming, "Do you really want to grow up and have to admit you never ran away?" Well, I guess I didn't because we did it. Trouble. I'll *never* forget that mistake.

As you're generating your own list, let your children begin generating theirs. I usually say, "As soon as you understand what I'm doing, take your pencil and begin working on your own list; you don't have to wait for me to finish." By my second or third topic, the kids are off and running.

FIGURE 1–2 Topic Sheet, Grade 1

We encourage first graders to draw pictures of their possible topics and to label their pictures with invented spelling (Figure 1–2).

Next, still using the overhead, we write (or draw) our favorite topic in the middle of a transparency, circle it, and then begin letting words that come into our mind flow onto the sheet. When we do this, we are showing children how to prepare a *cluster sheet*, one prewriting strategy we use frequently. We write slowly but deliberately. With first graders, we might only draw little figures around our topic.

FIGURE 1–3 Cluster Sheet About Marilyn

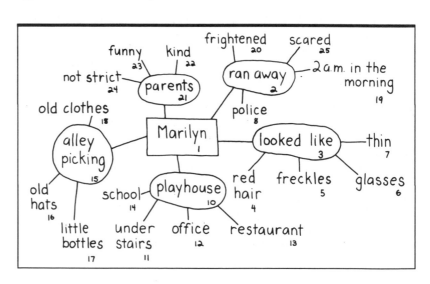

Figure 1–3 is my cluster sheet about Marilyn. (The numbers represent the order in which the words were written.) Since Marilyn had been one of my topics the day I wrote this, the children helped me do it. Not a bad idea, since they get right into the picture up front: they're doing the thinking along with you.

You will notice when looking at the numbers in the diagram that all the words related to a subtopic (i.e., "alley picking," "playhouse," "looked like," etc.) were not written before another subtopic came to mind. This is how prewriting works: one idea leads to another, then back again.

Believe it or not, even first graders can do this. However, in Matt's example (Figure 1–4) you will notice that the smaller circles are not connected in a logical way. For this reason we frequently draw, rather than cluster, with our first graders; it seems to depend on the class and the time of year.

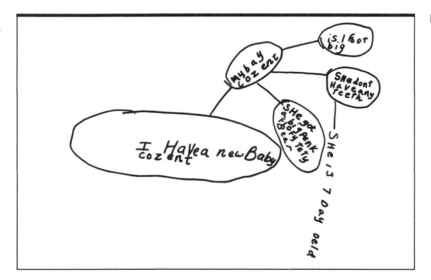

FIGURE 1–4 Matt, Grade 1

Figure 1–5 shows a cluster sheet prepared by a fourth grader about Harbor Springs, a resort area near her home.

Once you have finished this activity, let the children chat with a partner for a few minutes, with their cluster sheets (or drawings, in the case of some first graders) in hand. The children talk about what they have drawn or written, which gets language going in sentence form.

Then pass out some draft paper (we use either used computer paper; primer paper, the kind with a lot of wide lines; or small

FIGURE 1–5 Fourth Grader's Cluster Sheet

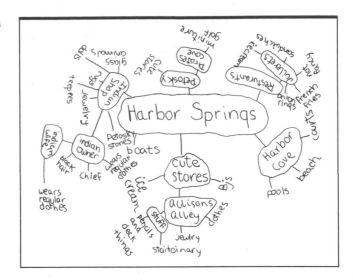

draft booklets) and begin writing. We encourage those who want to add to their drawing, or cluster sheet, to do so. Again, we write/draw on the overhead using a new transparency while the children write/draw at their desks. Everyone is quiet now and we insist on not being disturbed.

After about five minutes, we leave the overhead and begin walking around the room to help any children in trouble. Usually a simple question centering on some aspect of their cluster sheet or picture is enough to get a youngster moving along.

After about fifteen minutes, bring the children, with their drafts, to a corner of the room where you have set up two chairs, a child's chair and a large one (we use ours). Have a few children in mind, and one by one ask them to share what they have written or drawn. Be sure to guide your first reader to the *larger* chair, while you take the smaller one. (This puts the child, literally, on top of her world, even if only for a few minutes.) After you have told the author how you felt hearing the draft and you have mentioned something specific you liked, encourage the other children to tell the author how *they* felt when they heard the piece and what they liked or remembered. Then encourage a few children to ask the author questions.

The sharing of drafts can be modeled in an all-classroom conference. Here's a short excerpt from the audio tape I made on the day I wrote about Marilyn with the fourth graders. First, my written draft:

We loved alley picking, Marilyn and I, so that was usually a part of our Saturday morning ritual. We had alleys back then, mysterious, narrow dirt roads that wound behind our neat little houses with their man-icured lawns and apple trees, roads loaded with treasures just for the picking: belt buckles and old hats; stuffed chairs; old mason jars; min-iature bottles; wooden boxes; hat boxes all satin and shiny, laden with silk threads and stuffed with sweet-smelling tissue, pink usually; fake jewelry, gaudy as all getout; and sample wallpaper books by the dozen. We had fun hunting and sorting and figuring out what to take and what to leave behind for the others. We never left much.

Next, an excerpt of the class conversation about my draft:

Jody: I loved your list, all the things you used to pick up—the belt buckles and stuff.

Me: Yes, one day we dared each other to wear what we had found to school. What a riot. We did it and the other kids thought we were nuts.

Carol: I liked, "We never left much." You were mean. Did all the kids go alley picking?

Me: No, but a whole lot of us did. We'd fight over stuff, but I haven't gotten to *that* yet. I will, though. Does anybody have any other questions?

Susan: Did you really do that—alley picking, I mean?

Me: Yep. What do *you* do on Saturdays?

Susan: Watch TV, sometimes. Sometimes I go to my friend's house though. We play with her computer. Sometimes we build forts outside— when it's winter.

Me: You know, you could write about that.

Susan: Maybe.

Continue this routine of writing followed by all-class sharing for at least two to three weeks until each child has written on several topics. Once a number of drafts have been completed (any number more than one; but perhaps just one for your reluctant writers or for writers who have long drafts), choose a single draft for publication. Let us put off publication for just a bit, though, and describe a typical writing day later in the year, a day that will come sooner than you think.

BEYOND DAY ONE: A TYPICAL DAY

The nature of the writing period begins to change as the year progresses. We don't need to spend lots of time helping children generate topics, for example. Also, the children are beginning to confer with each other during conference time, what until now we've called all-class sharing. In reality, the all-class sharing was to prepare the children for conferencing on their own with a classmate or a small group.

By now our writing periods are usually forty-five minutes long (see Figure 1–6): fifteen minutes for *writing*, twenty minutes for holding *conferences* (what used to be all-class sharing during the first few weeks), and ten minutes for *sharing* either published drafts, writing strategies and observations, or teacher-directed, short, focused lessons (to be described in Section 2 of this book).

We should note here that the order—writing, holding conferences, and sharing/collegial chatter/focused teaching—frequently changes. This is because exciting things happen when children become writers. First grader Eric, for instance, came bursting in one day wanting to talk about chapters. He had discovered this "neat idea" (chapters!) for an information book he had just finished. Naturally, we had to have share time right away—to wait would have been ridiculous. After he showed the children the book he had discovered chapters in, the kids were

FIGURE 1–6 Writing Period

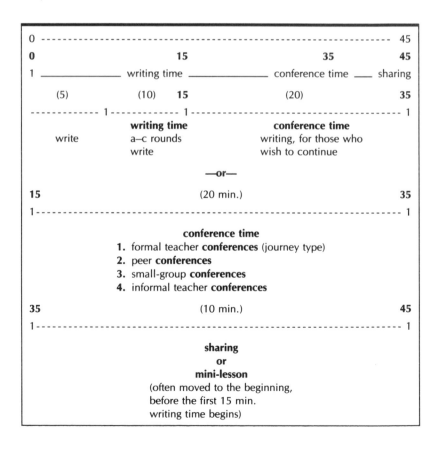

buzzing. (Some even began "chapter" books that day!) Sometimes the kids want to hear a story before writing time begins, especially first graders. Char Hahn, a first-grade teacher in Bloomfield Hills, Michigan, loves to start writing time this way. Why not? Kids get great ideas from books.

Though the order of when we have writing time, conference time, and share/teaching time changes, in the upper grades we *usually* begin each writing period with everyone writing, including the teacher (for about five minutes before rounds). We, as well as our children, need a chance to get in touch with our own writing processes. What's more, children need to see us write.

As on the first day, we suggest you then walk around the room, talking briefly with a few of your students, the ones you believe may need you the most. It helps if you have taken time the night before to review your children's writing folders. *Hunt for youngsters having problems.* Watch for either very little writing or for drafts that look extremely scribbled up or holey. Consider such marks or a lack of writing as clues to children in trouble, and choose these children for your early rounds. Sometimes writers in trouble just need a few minutes of your undivided attention. Giving this needed attention early in the day helps: you will have let these youngsters know that you care; and you *may*, incidentally, prevent unwanted interruptions later on. Another trick we use to detect children in need of us is to give each one a large circle at the beginning of the year. The children display these circles if they want us to stop by their desks during this quiet period, a period we sometimes call rounds.

After you have circulated among your students, call four to six children to the conference table. Since it helps children to know what they are going to say, consider assigning them to certain days. That is, specific children may be assigned to Mondays, others Tuesdays, and so on. Alternatively, you may choose to have a conference box in your room. When a child has a draft that she needs to share with you, as opposed to sharing it with a peer, the youngster may put her draft in the general conference box. We signify "general" because later, when children are publishing, we have several conference boxes, marked for specific purposes.

While some children are holding conferences with you, the other children should continue writing. (It might seem impossible to keep twenty or thirty children busy while you're holding conferences, but it's not. By the end of this section you will understand just how busy your children will be. Trust us for right now.) As the year progresses, the class members with whom you are not in conference may do other things as well. For example, children may:

1. continue writing/illustrating,
2. hold peer conferences or a group conference,
3. illustrate a piece for someone else,
4. read to another child from the author's chair, or
5. write with a friend.

By "write with a friend" we mean that sometimes children enjoy sitting next to someone special. Here's an excerpt from two first-grade friends talking with one another as they write. (For your reference, we've put their drafts before their dialogue.)

Jeff's Draft

Myfaziutmpar Trasr Maps
    Beeckuzzzazz
Zqa Leed to Trazzquas HrD Trazzrr
    maps

Ben's Draft

win I wnt to trontow and
I saw a clammttosor and it
had a gold tan and it
can soar big anamls and lill
anamls
it is osoo a plant
etre

Jeff: Okay, want to hear my radio?

Ben: Why don't you make a ghost right there?

Jeff [*reads*]: "My favorite treasure maps." Wait a minute, hold on. "My favorite treasure maps . . . My favorite maps are treasure maps because they lead to treasures." Now I got to write maps, don't I?

Ben: Now it's my turn. [*reading*] "When I went to Toranto and I saw a chlamydosaur. It had a golden tongue. And it can scare big animals and little animals. It is also a plant eater."

Jeff: Now what you should do is like make a room to act like it's really real. Okay?

Ben: You should make one like I'm makin' mine.

Jeff: I am. You should call it a meat eater. This is Jeffrey calling in. Our story today is about graveyard treasure maps. [*singing*] One star in the morning. One star tonight . . .

Ben: What are you singing?

Jeff: A code for my story.

Ben: Ha! Ha!

It's obvious from eavesdropping on Ben and Jeff collaborating that they are having the best of times. Their imaginary worlds blossom as they read and reread, write, and help one other shape their respective realities: "Now what you should do is like make a room to act like it's really real." And look at how gently Jeff suggests this to Ben: "Okay?" he asks, so as not to appear to take over his work. Oh, that we as teachers could be so gentle! We would surely make writers out of everyone.

Conference time, the noisy time we've been describing, where all the Bens and Jeffs are doing their own thing, usually lasts about twenty minutes. Because it's during conference time that we are able to work a bit longer with children *individually* (that is, longer than during rounds), we often wish it lasted longer. But there are lots of things to get done in school these days (probably too many), so we generally have to make do with the twenty or twenty-five minutes we've allotted. To help your individual conferences run smoothly, we offer this suggestion: *Read your children's drafts the night before*. This will make the biggest difference in terms of time well spent. Beginning a conference unprepared will naturally result in a less efficient meeting.

The last few minutes of every writing day (or sometimes the first few) we spend sharing or teaching a short, focused lesson (see Section 2 for detailed examples of focused lessons). Sharing drafts is important. Children get support from one another, new directions in which to take their work, ideas for endings, and so on. It astounds us, every day, how invaluable children are to one another, how they go beyond us, magnificently, in drawing each other out as learners. Watch how Christen's classmates bring their own experience to her, on a silver platter, if you will; and how their experiences enrich hers by causing her to think about her life, her experiences. Her classmates help themselves, as well, by quickly assessing the situation before they speak, drawing from their prior knowledge, assimilating what they've heard (as they'll do someday when they read), and moving on beyond her reality into their own. Listen while Mrs. Allan's first graders hear and respond to Christen's draft about cooking. Christen reads:

Cooking is fun.
my mom helps me.
And it is very fun.

So I cook good sotf [stuff]
And my family
Loves it and I do to.

Christen: Any comments or questions? Laura.

Laura: Does your mom let you cook every day?

Christen: Yes, she does. Tyler.

Tyler: Can you reach the place where you turn on the stove? 'Cause I can't.

Christen: It's low, it's very low. Seth.

Seth: Why is there a stamp on that like? [*There's a 22-cent stamp on the page, above her drawing.*]

Christen: I don't know.

Teacher: Do you know what he's talking about?

Christen [*Shrugs off the question*]: Jessica.

Jessica: What do you cook sometimes?

Christen: Macaroni, psghetti, and steak.

Student: Psghetti?? [*laughter over her pronunciation*]

Teacher: That's what happens when you have a loose tooth.

Christen: Ryan.

Ryan: I have a cookbook too.

Christen: I have a special cookbook for my dad. He's got a low-calorie cookbook.

Ryan: I have a special one too, something like it. It has mostly teddy bears in it. It can get you lunch, breakfast, and dinner.

Teacher: What about the teddy bears, Ryan?

Ryan: That's for . . . um . . . dessert or something, I don't know. . . .

Christen: Johnny.

Johnny: I have a cookbook, too.

Christen: Is it like a special kind of cookbook, or is it just a regular one?

Johnny: It's special. [*Of course!*]

Teacher: How is yours special?

Johnny: It gots low calories, like Christen's.

Christen: Wendy.

Wendy: Do you read your cookbook, or does your mom?

Christen: My mom does and she tells me what to put in. Amy.

Amy: I have little cards that tells me how to cook. And all it'll do is desserts and stuff, like cookies.

Christen: Yes. That's the recipe cards. Sometimes my mom writes 'em and sometimes my grandma writes 'em.

Tell me, would any of us have done any better as Christen's conference partner? I doubt that we would have ever asked, "Can you reach the place where you turn on the stove?" or mentioned those "little cards."

Before closing this section on a typical day, we would like to add a note on generating topics and how this changes as the year progresses. The children get stuck in a rut at times. What shall they write about? Don't be alarmed. When this happens we usually bring in a stack of good books and think together about possibilities. For example, last week this happened in a second-grade class I visit. I went to the library and pulled these books off the shelf: *Owl Moon* (Yolan, 1987), *The Pain and the Great One* (Blume, 1985), *The Good-Bye Book* (Viorst, 1988), and *Whale Song* (Johnson, 1987). The exact books don't matter, it's just the idea that published books can give us ideas. Using Jane Yolan's *Owl Moon*, for example, I simply asked the children if they had ever been taught to do something by a parent or grandparent. "Oh, yes," they replied.

"I've been taught to empty the dishwasher," Janie said. Mark told us his grandpa taught him how to whittle. I explained to the children that Jane Yolan's father taught her how to go owling and that she wrote a book about it.

The children catch on right away and begin adding to their topic lists. I pull the next book off my lap, *The Pain and the Great One*, and begin again. "How many of you have a brother or sister?" Soon we were talking about Judy Blume's use of two voices.

Again, the point in all this is to help children discover topics. We find literature a fine, topic-generating tool; we urge you to try it.

SUGGESTIONS FOR SETTING UP THE CLASSROOM

The Classroom

We have never needed very much: a lot of paper; colored markers and pencils; a folder/binder for each child, complete with pockets and clips for holding papers, to house work in progress; a manila folder for everyone, to hold already published or unwanted drafts; some colorful baskets, which we number to accommodate the steps that drafts go through on their way toward publication; an author's chair that the children use whenever they read their work (Graves and Hansen, 1983); some bulletin board space to celebrate our authors or to depict the writing process; at least one round table for group conferences, whether teacher led or child led; a bookshelf to house our ever-growing classroom library; and a typewriter or computer to print out our final drafts.

Most classrooms have these materials, or things similar, available to them as part of the school budget. An author's chair can be found at a garage sale and bookshelves can be makeshift, if need be. The point is, you shouldn't need much. Two luxuries we allow ourselves, however, are pads of stick-on note paper and a rubber stamp that says DRAFT. The sticky pads allow us to record all sorts of information for authors, or let authors take their own notes, freeing them to place the sheet wherever they need it on their draft. (An adhesive stick, which is new on the market, can turn any ordinary piece of scratch paper into a tack-a-note.) The DRAFT stamp encourages young authors to write freely, without worrying about mechanical, grammatical, or spelling errors. Drafts are just that, drafts, and the DRAFT stamp proves it!

The Writing Folder

Works in progress have to be housed in a folder/binder, and we use ones with pockets and center clips. When open, they look like Figure 1–7. The left hand pocket holds topic and cluster sheets, and the right hand side holds drafts in progress. We save the center for our ever-growing writing manual.

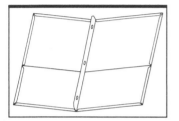

FIGURE 1–7 Writing Folder

Topic Sheet

We've tried all types of topic sheet, but we find ones similar to the one in Figure 1–8 work the best. Children fill in their names on day one and then, as topics occur to them, they write them down right on their topic sheets. When they choose a topic to write on, they fill in the square under the number. Josh's is shown in Figure 1–9.

First-grade teachers might prefer fewer spaces for topics, like the one in Figure 1–10. You will notice that this topic sheet has several triangles beneath each number, whereas the previous topic sheet has only one square. The teacher who designed this topic sheet told us many children like writing on the same topic several times, hence she added more triangles (she preferred triangles to squares).

A second option for first-grade teachers is to simply fold a piece of manila paper in half and have the children draw two possibilities. Option three is to forget topic lists altogether. Char Hahn does, believing that first graders have no trouble spontaneously delivering good ideas for writing.

Cluster Sheet

As we've discussed, one way to engage children in prewriting is through the use of cluster sheets. Some children don't want to

```
              TOPICS
            Your Name_____
1.              7.
 □               □
-------------------------------
2.              8.
 □               □
-------------------------------
3.              9.
 □               □
-------------------------------
4.              10.
 □               □
-------------------------------
5.              11.
 □               □
-------------------------------
6.              12.
 □               □
```

FIGURE 1–8 Topic Sheet

```
              TOPICS
            Your Name_____
1.              7.
 □  bike rideing  Kivin
2.              8.
 □  seleing      □  socer
3.              9.
 □  goldfish  □ fishing
4.              10.
 □  skoll      □  ▒▒▒
5.              11.
 □  pano    □ t. chess
6.              12.
 □               □
```

FIGURE 1–9 Josh's Topic Sheet

```
   Topics      Name_____
   _____

1.
   ▲▲▲▲
   - - - - - - - - - - - - -
2.
   ▲▲▲▲
   - - - - - - - - - - - - -
3.
   ▲▲▲▲
   - - - - - - - - - - - - -
4.
   ▲▲▲▲
```

FIGURE 1–10 First-Grade Topic Sheet

use them, preferring to draw, while many children find them helpful. Like pictures, a cluster sheet serves as a memory bank for young authors. Figure 1–11 is one type of cluster sheet.

We cannot overemphasize the importance of the phrase "*one type of cluster sheet*," nor can we emphasize enough the notion that other prewriting strategies abound. A group of third graders recently produced the list in Figure 1–12.

```
                        Name _____




        ⬭
```

FIGURE 1–11 Cluster Sheet

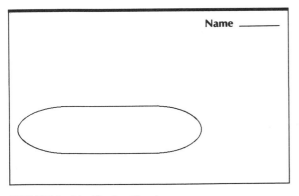

Pre-Writing Ideas

1. Brainstorming - 🖼
2. pictures 🖼 or doodle 🖼
3. List of words 🗒
4. Read and take notes 📖 📑
5. Interview Someone 🧍🧍
6. Mind Mapping 🗺 swimming, showr on my bike, sleep, bath

FIGURE 1–12 A Third-Grade List: "Pre-Writing Ideas"

The Manual

A writer's manual for elementary children isn't going to be very detailed. Nevertheless, there are guideline sheets and resource material sheets that we find helpful to have on hand. We don't pass the manual sheets out all at once (and a few teachers we work with don't use them at all). What follows are some suggestions of what to include in a writer's manual.

Figure 1–13, entitled "Things I Can Do During Writing Time," was designed with first and second graders in mind. It allows children to review their options before they begin writing. As the year progresses, children color in the little hands by the options that have been discussed and are in use at the time. Teachers vary on how they use this sheet—some allowing children to use all the possibilities at once, others going more slowly—but it has been our experience that many teachers use some sheet, in one form or another, to remind the children of their options. Mrs.

FIGURE 1–13 "What I Can Do During Writing Time"—Younger Version

```
Things  I  Can  Do  During  Writing  Time

☞1.  I  can  add  to  my  topic  list.  ✛

☞2.  I  can  brainstorm  a  new  topic.

☞3.  I  can  begin  a  new  draft.

☞4.  I  can  improve  or  add  on  to  a
        draft  I  have  started.

☞5.  I  can  draw  some  pictures  for  one
        of  my  drafts.

☞6.  I  can  underline  misspelled  words.
        (This  is  proofreading.)

☞7.  I  can  look  for  words  that  should
        be  capitalized.
        (This  is  also  proofreading.)

☞8.  I  can  read  my  drafts  to  myself
        and  decide  which  one  I  want  to
        publish.
```

Things To Do During **Writing Time**

1. Add to or revise a current draft.

2. Edit a draft for the problems you can see.

3. Brainstorm a topic from your topic list or gather information.

4. Think about topics for your topic list.

5. Write about what you did yesterday—to help you find a topic.

6. Draw pictures to go with your article or book.

Things To Do During **Conference Time**

1. One through Six above.

2. Hold a conference with one of your friends or your teacher.

3. Be in a group conference.

4. Help a friend draw pictures for his or her book, if you are asked.

5. Write with a friend.

Types of **Peer/Group** Conferences

1. Topic Conference: Explore one of your topics with your partner(s). Try and discover what is most important to you. Or, gather information for a new topic with a friend.

2. Draft Conference: Meet with your partner(s) if you're stuck in the middle of your draft. Ask your partner(s) for ideas on how you might move on. Or, just share a draft with a friend.

3. Revision Conference: See "Conference Questions," and use one of these with your partner(s). (Or, make up another question to suit your needs.) Follow your conference guidelines.

4. Editing Conference: Edit for something from the "Proofreading Checklist" that you are not good at spotting yourself.

5. Publishing Conference: (a) Read one of your published works to your partner(s). (b) Work on dividing an edited, polished draft for publication (typists need to know where to stop and start).

FIGURE 1–14 "What I Can Do During Writing Time"— Older Version

Brown's first-grade class dictated this list to her: think up topics, draw pictures and write, work on a draft you started already, cut out pictures to put in your writing folder. Mrs. Brown highly approved, telling the children they were free to write with a friend as well.

Older children in many of our classrooms use a variation of the younger children's version (Figure 1–14).

The sheet in Figure 1–15, entitled "Things I Can Do During Conference Time," is also a popular one because, like its predecessor, it lets the children know what they may do. Unlike the quieter nature (in many classrooms, not all) of writing-time activities, most of the conference-time activities involve interaction. You will note that writing is still an option during conference

FIGURE 1–15 "Things I Can
Do During Conference Time"

Things I Can Do During Conference Time

☞1. I can do anything from my <u>Writing
       Time</u> list.

☞2. I can hold a conference with a
       friend.☺ or ☺☺

☞3. I can write with a
       friend. ⌇☺⌇☺⌇☺⌇☺⌇☺⌇

☞4. I can draw some pictures for one
       of my friend's drafts.✎✎✎

☞5. I can hold a conference with my
       teacher. 🦱 or 🧑

time, that period when conferences are permitted and talking is
encouraged. Children especially love option number three: writing with a friend. They either pull their desks together or crawl
under a nearby table with their drafts.

In addition to the writing-time and conference-time sheets,
we include a sheet outlining simple conference guidelines in the
manual (see Figure 1–16). Do you recall in the section on what
to do on the first day how we modeled sharing during what was
to become conference time later on? The conference guidelines
here are nothing more than that, our sharing strategy written
down. During conference time children may share their work, no
matter what stage their drafts are in. But there are guidelines.
Although the children are free to meander from our formula when
they need to, the guidelines do provide a *starting point* for peer
interaction.

Older children soon advance to a more sophisticated guideline sheet that encourages the author to select what she wants a
group or partner to listen for (Figure 1–17).

FIGURE 1–16 Conference
Guidelines—Simple

1. Listen to your partner's draft.
2. Tell your partner what you liked about the draft, what you thought was inter-
    esting, or how you felt as you listened to it.
3. Listen to your partner's draft again.
4. If you have a question about your partner's topic, this is a good time to ask it.
    (If you have time, write your question down and give it to your partner. This
    will help your partner remember what you asked.)

CONFERENCE GUIDELINES: Listening with a purpose in mind

(Feel free to start at step #3 if you'd like.)

1. Read your draft to your partner.

2. Let your partner tell you what he or she remembers the most about your piece (i.e., What was interesting or what sounded good?).

3. Read your draft again, but this time ask your partner to listen for Conference Question(s) # _____ and/or # _____.

4. Let your partner respond to what you asked him or her to listen for. Your partner may give you other worthwhile suggestions. Listen carefully.

5. Remember, *you* are the author. Suggestions that others give you may be helpful, but they may *not* be. Change only those parts of your draft that you feel need changing.

CONFERENCE QUESTIONS: A few possibilities

1. Listen to my opening line(s). Does my lead interest you? If not, how might I improve it?

2. Do you think I need more information anywhere? That is, are there places in my draft where you would like me to get more specific? Where?

3. Do you ever get lost while reading/listening to my draft? When?

4. Do I get too wordy in my draft? That is, have I put in too much detail ("deadwood")? Where?

5. Have I mentioned things in my draft (for example, people, actions, or situations) that are hard for you to picture, *that you wish you could picture*? What are they?

6. Do you think that the sentences/paragraphs in my draft are in the best order possible? If not, which sentences/paragraphs would you move around? Why?

7. Do you think I should let my feelings/inner thoughts show more in places? Where?

8. Do I stay on my topic?

9. Do I have a good ending? If not, do you have a suggestion for how I might improve it?

10. Does my title fit my draft?

Other Possibilities

11.

12.

13.

14.

15.

16.

FIGURE 1–17 Conference Guidelines—Advanced

FIGURE 1–18 Listener's Guide to a Peer or Group Conference

YOUR NAME _____   Date _____

CONFERENCE WITH: _____

THEIR STORY TITLE/TOPIC _____

What I liked or thought was interesting:

_____

_____

_____

_____

_____

What I would like to know more about:

_____

_____

_____

_____

_____

_____

Suggestions for improvement:

_____

_____

_____

_____

_____

As with everything else, we model peer conferences several times before we expect the children to confer with each other. Some of us have our older children use a listener's guide (see Figure 1–18) during peer conferences to keep them on task.

Here is a draft written by Sherry, a fifth-grade student of Mr. Myers from Dublin Elementary in Walled Lake, Michigan.

On Halloween night with vampires,
gost, mummys, and warlocks,
I saw a old scary house.
I walked up to it and went in.
They was no one in site.
I walk over to the kichen,

but no one was there.

I saw something with vampire teeth,
it scared me I ran as fast as

I could in the living room and
saw a warlock.

I ran out side and went home.

THE END

We put Sherry's draft on an overhead transparency (with her permission, of course) and transferred the listener's guide questions right onto the overhead. What follows are the comments, questions, and suggestions her classmates had for her:

What I liked or thought was interesting:

Your handwriting fits the mood, especially "THE END."
Your topic wasn't any old night, it was Halloween. Good topic!
You rhymed a little bit—"night/sight."
You used lots of Halloween words.
I liked the way you opened up, "On Halloween night with vampires,
    ghosts, mummies, and warlocks, I saw an old scary house."
You "ran" into the living room. That was good.
You really set a scary mood, I felt creepy inside at first.

What I would like to know more about:

What did you do when you got home?
What's a warlock?
What was her name?
Can you describe the characters more, I mean the vampire and the
    warlock and the mummy?
Could you tell me more about how you were scared?
How did you get past all those creatures? Did they chase you?
Can you describe the house more? What did it look like?
Did she ever return?

Suggestions for improvement:

You might want to draw a picture to go with your poem.
In general, I think you need to work a little more on your ending. I'm
    not sure though, it's up to you.

Of course, Sherry didn't use all the questions and suggestions as she revised her draft, just the ones she thought would add to the quality of her work. It's important that children know "questions" and "suggestions" are *possible* points of departure for revision, not mandates. In fact, sometimes children don't use them at all. The trick, as a teacher of young people, is to know when not to butt in. Sometimes, during one of your teacher-child conferences, you'll feel driven to push *a little too far*—to get just one more "great" idea *of yours* across. Don't do it (though you probably will at first). Why? Because our children will grow as writers as long as they love to write and as long as they write a lot. As soon as we start pushing our ideas on them, they feel a loss of ownership. And how can they resist us? After all, we *are* their teacher. Remember, it is one thing to respond as an interested reader and teacher to a youngster's piece, but another thing altogether when we want to hear our voice in the draft.

We like what Tom Romano (1987) says about teacher feedback in his wonderful book, *Clearing the Way: Working with Teenage Writers*. Romano's comments and grades are "calculated to induce the student to write again." We've used one of Romano's comments as a sort of teacher guideline for conferences: Stop "suggesting" before you lose your audience.

To bring closure to the writing period, sometimes we use a writing log, which is also part of the manual. Figure 1–19 is one example. Children write in these eagerly, so teachers go through the folders periodically and read them. Fundamentally, however, the logs are meant for the children, to chronicle their own writing behavior. A typical example reads, "I had a hard time getting started today, but I wrote a lot, finally. Jason helped me."

THE DYNAMICS OF MOVING ALONG A DRAFT TO BE PUBLISHED
Grades Two Through Six

Publishing children's work is an important part of process-writing classrooms, but because children write so much, we find we cannot publish everything. This state of affairs is probably healthy. After all, professional writers don't attempt to publish every draft they produce: *everything* isn't good enough. For professionals, what they choose to submit is usually a matter of choice; and so, perhaps, it should be for children.

Right from the beginning of the year the children are told that some of their work will be published, but some will not. Every time they have completed a certain number of drafts on separate topics, perhaps two or three, maybe even four, *they* are to choose one and send it on a publishing journey. (Of course, the number of required drafts depends on the child and the cir-

FIGURE 1–19 Writing Log

Name _____

Date	What I Did Today	How Today Went Great OK Slow Moving

cumstances: slow writers might publish *every* draft; long drafts needn't wait; commemorative drafts have publication deadlines; etc.) We explain that professional writers must send drafts on journeys too, often mailing their work back and forth several times. Children have no problem understanding this, and they eagerly await our explanation and instructions to guide their foray into publishing. This is what we tell them.

"When you have selected your best draft, we would like you to make a publishing packet, with your draft sandwiched in between a journey sheet and a proofreading checklist. Sandwiched might sound kind of funny, but listen carefully. Your *draft* will be like the peanut butter or the tuna fish you would use if you were making a sandwich: it will be your filling. Your top piece of bread will be a journey sheet [see Figure 1–20] and your bottom piece of bread will be a proofreading sheet [see Figure 1–21]. Use the stapler and staple your sandwich together, at the top. Then, follow the instructions on your journey sheet and send your draft on its way." (Some experts find the term *sandwich* condescending. It has never hit us this way, but you may prefer a different term, perhaps *publishing packet*.)

Though we will talk about this journey sheet (Figure 1–20) as if it were the only one, in truth they are as varied as the teachers themselves. This one was designed by Betty Morris, a second-grade teacher in Birmingham, Michigan, with me. After outlining Betty's and mine, we will show you four others, three designed by teachers, one by a sixth-grade class.

Looking through the journey sheet, you'll notice the first thing a child is asked to do after choosing a draft is to write the date on the journey sheet (Step 1). Then, the youngster reads his draft to a friend (Step 2). Since writing time is a quiet time, conference time is the period for sharing. (During writing time, this child would have to work on another draft, or reread this one.)

After conferring with a friend, our youngster will work on revising his piece *if he needs to* (Step 3). We find that children ask their peers questions all the time, and many youngsters opt to add on after their conference sessions. Here are several questions a classmate asked Marcia, the second-grade author of the draft on witches (see Figure 1–22):

1. How do you know all of this?
2. What do they do when the bats perch on their noses?
3. Can you describe the stubs?
4. How come they have the power of 300 strong men?

FIGURE 1–20 Journey Sheet

PUBLISHING JOURNEY

Name _____ Grade _____
Date

1. Choose a draft you would like to publish. _____

2. Read your draft to a friend. Use your conference guidelines. _____

3. Work on your draft if you need to. Add some information, or move words around. _____

4. Try editing your draft by yourself. _____
   (a) Underline any words you think are misspelled.
   (b) Look for capitals, periods, or other punctuation you may need. (Use your editing pencil.)

5. Put your draft in **Conference Box 1**. _____
   This is when we read and share together. I will point to interesting things I remember, and I may ask you some questions in order to learn what you have to teach me. Then you will work on your draft if you need to.

6. Hold another peer conference. Use your conference guidelines. _____

7. Put your draft in **Conference Box 2**. _____
   During this conference we will look at your editing and discuss at least one new skill you may need to learn to complete your piece. Then you will work on your piece.

8. Recopy your draft if you need to. _____
   (You only need to recopy your draft if it is too hard to read.)

9. Put your draft in our **Pre-Publishing Box**. _____
   During this conference, one of our aides or I will ask you how you want to finish your book. (For example: How many pages do you want? Where will each page start and stop? Where do you think you may want your pictures? What would you like on your cover? Do you want an "About The Author" page?)

10. Put your draft in our **To Be Published Box**. _____
    After I have looked at your draft one last time, you will recopy it on publishing paper or we will send it to a typist.

11. Day book was completed _____

Marcia kept track of these questions, which were written on the sticky paper we mentioned earlier, and worked some, but not all, of the answers into her draft.

Step 4, editing the draft, is a helpful step for two reasons: Teachers like knowing their children respect them enough to give them readable work, and children benefit from attempting to edit alone. We ask our students to use red pencils when they edit so we can celebrate their discoveries with them.

Once Step 4 has been completed, children put their "sandwiches" in Conference Box 1 (Step 5). Papers in this box are now ready for us to read.

FIGURE 1–21 Proofreading Checklist

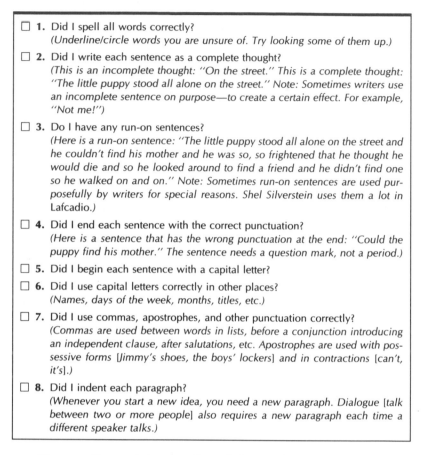

☐ **1.** Did I spell all words correctly?
(Underline/circle words you are unsure of. Try looking some of them up.)

☐ **2.** Did I write each sentence as a complete thought?
(This is an incomplete thought: "On the street." This is a complete thought: "The little puppy stood all alone on the street." Note: Sometimes writers use an incomplete sentence on purpose—to create a certain effect. For example, "Not me!")

☐ **3.** Do I have any run-on sentences?
(Here is a run-on sentence: "The little puppy stood all alone on the street and he couldn't find his mother and he was so, so frightened that he thought he would die and so he looked around to find a friend and he didn't find one so he walked on and on." Note: Sometimes run-on sentences are used purposefully by writers for special reasons. Shel Silverstein uses them a lot in Lafcadio.)

☐ **4.** Did I end each sentence with the correct punctuation?
(Here is a sentence that has the wrong punctuation at the end: "Could the puppy find his mother." The sentence needs a question mark, not a period.)

☐ **5.** Did I begin each sentence with a capital letter?

☐ **6.** Did I use capital letters correctly in other places?
(Names, days of the week, months, titles, etc.)

☐ **7.** Did I use commas, apostrophes, and other punctuation correctly?
(Commas are used between words in lists, before a conjunction introducing an independent clause, after salutations, etc. Apostrophes are used with possessive forms [Jimmy's shoes, the boys' lockers] and in contractions [can't, it's].)

☐ **8.** Did I indent each paragraph?
(Whenever you start a new idea, you need a new paragraph. Dialogue [talk between two or more people] also requires a new paragraph each time a different speaker talks.)

We usually read four or five of them after school, in preparation for the formal teacher-child conferences we will hold the next day, or on the next writing day. (We refer to these as *formal* conferences, because during our daily rounds we often talk with children informally about their drafts.)

The first conference we hold with a child centers on meaning. We frequently tell them how their draft makes us feel and point to interesting parts of the draft. Sometimes we ask the child to identify the part(s) that works best for her. If a piece isn't too long, we may ask the youngster to read the whole draft out loud. Just hearing a child read her piece gives us information about what we should do next. For the sake of clarity, rather than going into teacher-child conferencing techniques now, we will defer this discussion to our conferencing section and move on to Step 6 of the journey sheet. One last comment before we do. At the end of Conference 1 we ask the children to look over the Proofreading

All witchtes are very ugly. They have long gren Bumpy noises, and some Bats might purtch on it. Witch noseslook like there made of paper mashy. They have wiges with sowigly measy hair on them. They are all BalD and wair masks, Becaus they have stu Bs. They have Black cat's with Gloewing green eyes. They alse have monsters what they keep in cages chaned to walls. They feed them Banana peals and They also eat long sticks of Butter. Witches' sleep on sement flowers. They alwes wear capes, hats and Dark Black clower. There head's a shaped like Onions, and Smell like Skunks. And There head's are as fragle as mash qatartos. Same wirches are geod But Most are Bad. Witches have the pawe of Soo Strong men from the Circes. They are very strong and have the magic of 79 Miqishons. They can tur into the tallest Giant To the Smalest fly. Witphes eat flys and Slime. And there favret Dish is spider wibe pie, with honey on top. The good witches are very, Very good, and very, very, nice. But witches eat childrer with a Bit of Salt and a Bit of Pepar. They have a specl masheen. It's a Bike with the Back wheel in a pot with Baling hot water. And Knives Stalded in to yeu way Down, deep. You peadel And the Back whel and it mikkes you the Salt, Pepar a your Blod. And that Tastes Better than Spider wibe pie with honey on to.

FIGURE 1–22 Marcia's "All Witches" Draft

Checklist (Figure 1–21) and mark the editing skills they think they can use by themselves. This way, before putting their drafts in Conference Box 2 (where we deal with proofreading), they have had an opportunity to try their hand at editing *once again*. Several second graders will check off numbers four and six; many have already completed number one; older children check many more. Again, the children are asked to use red pencils, so that we can see which improvements they were able to make without our help.

Step 6 calls for another peer conference. The more interaction young authors have with an audience, the better. This is because children are egocentric: they aren't quite aware of what their audience knows and doesn't know, nor of what their audience needs to understand in order to comprehend the message. (Our early drafts are egocentric, as well.) Consequently, the journey sheet provides many opportunities for interaction. (Children may not want to hold another peer conference; we often tell them they may skip this conference if they'd like to.)

Our second formal conference with a child is an editing conference. During this second editing conference (Step 7), we look at how well they have corrected what they said they could manage. If they haven't done a very good job, we help them with one of the skills they identified as being "known"; if they have found all of their errors, we celebrate this and then move on, teaching them one, and only one, *new* skill.

Once a child has edited as much as he can, we frequently do the rest alone, although sometimes we do this with the youngster nearby. We use *a different color pencil* when editing to tune us in to the skills we need to teach. Then, if the draft is readable, the piece moves on to the Pre-Publishing Box; if not, it has to be recopied (Step 8). We try and avoid Step 8 at all costs, especially with less mature children. During the pre-publishing conference (Step 9), we do little things, like decide on page breaks. If we are fortunate enough to have an aide or a volunteer parent on hand, he or she holds this conference with the child. Sometimes children from older grades help us; on the other hand, many children do this step alone.

When the draft is ready for publication, it moves on to Step 10 where it is placed in our publishing folder or box. It either gets sent to a typist—often a parent in the room—or the draft is recopied onto special publishing paper by the child or teacher (usually the child). The letter you see in Figure 1–23 is one a writing consultant sent to teachers who were initiating a process approach in their classrooms.

Several schools in which we work have a central clearinghouse for drafts that are to be published. Teams of parents collect these drafts periodically and type them, using school computers. Papers are sent to the office with a slip similar to the one in Figure 1–24, and drafts come back all typed and ready to be illustrated.

When a child's book is completed, which means it has been printed and illustrated, the date is written on the last line of the journey sheet, Step 11. This is a big day for a youngster, because he knows that soon he will be sitting in the author's chair sharing

Dear Teachers,

We are extremely fortunate to have five parents available to type for us. Here's how the system will work

1. Attach a "Publishing Request" form to each draft you'd like typed. (The forms are located over your mailbox in the office)

2. Fill out the form exactly as you wish it typed. Circle the type size you want.

3. Put the draft (with publishing request attached) into the metal box over your mailbox.

4. Your typed draft will be delivered to you.

Remember:
1. All drafts must be edited-completely
2. page breaks must be clearly visible (sample:)
3. State, by each page number, where you want the words typed
   t = top   m = middle   b = bottom
   c = centered over entire page

FIGURE 1–23 Sample Letter to Teachers

Publishing Request

Child's name _____

Date _____

Teacher _____

Type Size _____ 20 _____ 40 _____ 80

Typist's Signature _____

FIGURE 1–24 Publishing Request

his work with the class. And the class will clap when he's done and tell him about their favorite parts. Some will say, "I love your illustrations," some will comment on the parts of the story (poem, essay, etc.) they enjoyed the most. Others will wonder, "How did you think of all that?" while still others will wish they had written the book themselves, and they will say so.

As we have said earlier, the particular journey sheet we have led you through is just *one* example. Once teachers are aware of the journey concept, they often create their own. A first-grade teacher designed the one in Figure 1–25; a second-grade teacher, Kevin Keller of Walled Lake, Michigan, used some original graphics for his (see Figure 1–26); a collection of many teachers over two years have come up with Figure 1–27; and Mrs. Grahm's

---

First Grade Journey Sheet

Your name _____

Date _____

1. Read your draft to yourself. ☐

2. Read your draft to a friend. ☐

Whom did you read it to?_____

[Let your friend tell you what was great. Let your friend ask you questions.]

3. Put on your editing hat.
Edit your draft for
☐ spelling [Underline words that need help.]
☐ capitals [≡ƒ means make it a capital.
            ≠ƒ means make it lower case.]

4. Put your draft in our
Publishing Box. ☐

FIGURE 1–25 First-Grade Journey Sheet

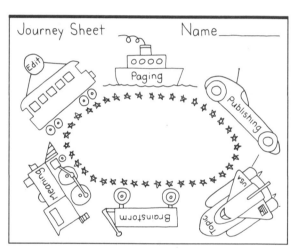

FIGURE 1–26 Kevin's Journey Sheet

FIGURE 1–27 Second-Through Sixth-Grade Journey Sheet

Your name _____

Date _____

Title _____

1. Read your draft to yourself. ☐ _____
   (You might: add words, take out words, check your sentence sense, add punc-tuation, find capitals, find spelling errors, etc.)

2. Read your draft **two** times to a friend. ☐ _____
   Whom did you read it to? _____
   (Remember: 1) Let your friend tell you what was great. 2) Let your friend ask you questions.)

   My friend's questions:

   _____

   _____

   _____

3. Revise.
   (For example, you might add information if you need to, omit repetitions, check your ending or your opening lines, check your sentence order, cross out all your extra "and"s, etc.) ☐ _____

4. Edit your draft for
   ☐ spelling   ☐ _____
   ☐ end punctuation   ☐ _____
   ☐ capital letters   ☐ _____

5. **Teacher Conference 1** ☐ _____

6. How will you publish: ☐ typed ☐ computer ☐ handwritten
   ☐ it will remain informal
   (stop after step 7)

7. Where will you publish? ☐ book ☐ class journal
   ☐ bulletin board ☐ loudspeaker ☐ class drama

8. **Final Teacher Check** ☐

9. Put your draft in our **Publishing Box**. ☐

sixth-grade class from Dublin Elementary in Walled Lake wrote the one in Figure 1–28. Again, please remember, some teachers do not use journey sheets at all.

Transitional First Grade and Young First Grade Classrooms: Two Approaches

Dorothy Bell's System.   Journey sheets work well in some class-rooms, but not all. Dorothy Bell, a transitional first-grade teacher, was frustrated—not even a journey sheet would help her. Six weeks before solving her publishing problem, things were getting

FIGURE 1–28 Journey Sheet from Mrs. Grahm's Sixth Grade

Choose Your Own Journey   Name _____

Topic _____

1. Choose a draft you want to publish. ☐ date(s) _____
2. Conference with a friend. ☐ date(s) _____
   ☐ How do you like it? (e.g., exciting, funny, sad, boring, interesting, etc.)
   ☐ What should I keep? ☐ What should I eliminate?
   ☐ Are there enough details? ☐ Too many details?
   ☐ Good beginning? ☐ Good ending?
   ☐ Good description ☐ Other
3. Fix it so that you like it! ☐ date(s) _____
4. Proofread: ☐ punctuation ☐ capitals ☐ paragraphs
   ☐ spelling ☐ unwanted run-ons or fragments
   date(s) _____
5. Teacher conference: date _____
   ☐ check proofreading
   ☐ check what I asked my friend to listen for
   ☐ check if it makes sense
   ☐ check for best word choice or overused words
   ☐ other _____
6. Final proofreading ☐ date(s) _____
7. Publish: ☐ type at home ☐ write it out ☐ computer
   date(s) _____
8. Design a cover: ☐ date(s) _____
9. Illustrate: ☐ date(s) _____
10. Write an "About the Author" page: ☐ yes ☐ no: date(s) _____

MY JOURNEY

☐ ☐ ☐ ☐ ☐ ☐ ☐ ☐ ☐ ☐

out of hand. The children could write, she knew that; they could invent their spelling; find their own topics; even share constructively. But the room was a mess. Kids were crawling out of the woodwork wanting her attention, this instant! And everyone wanted to publish—now.

Anyone who works with young children knows that that's the way it goes: there's no such thing as "sharing tomorrow" or "publishing tomorrow" for six-year-olds. But Dorothy needed "until tomorrow." If she didn't get a break, she might even give up.

Fortunately Dorothy isn't a giver-upper. One day after school Dorothy sat down to figure the whole thing out. She thought of a way to handle her classroom so that she could do all the things she wanted to do: listen to her children read their drafts, talk to them about their topics, celebrate their accomplishments with

FIGURE 1–29 A Topic Sheet

enthusiasm, and publish their work. What follows is a step-by-step account of Dorothy's classroom setup.

First of all, Dorothy wanted her children to choose their own topics; she knew that good writing begins this way. But the topic lists that teachers of older youngsters had given her, sheets with lots of numbers and blank spaces for ideas, weren't right. Her children got confused. So Dorothy decided that she would ask her children to think of a few topics at a time. She would give them each a piece of construction paper, have them fold it in half, and then she would ask them to draw a picture of two possible topics, one on each side of the paper. (They could include more if they wanted to, but she didn't press for more.) Dorothy would model this first, and then ask her students to do it. (Figure 1–29 is a topic sheet.)

Next, Dorothy would ask them to choose one of their topics and go to the writing center, where she would have paper ready. The paper would be special, however. Its size would be one half the size of the paper she would use for publication:

<table>
<tr><td>draft
paper</td><td>publishing
paper</td></tr>
</table>

Dorothy reasoned that when the children recopied their work (using conventional spelling), she would have room to paste their original writing (which was done using invented spelling) in the upper right hand corner of the corrected version. Why include the invented spelling version in the published draft? Because Dorothy knew that her youngsters might not be able to read the conventional spelling right now, but she hoped they would be able to in a few months; in fact, she was counting on it.

Dorothy tried out everything she dreamed up. When her children finished writing their first rough drafts, she asked them to get a manila folder from the writing center and place the draft inside. If she wasn't busy, she'd listen right away; but if she was, she'd ask them to put their draft in the folder and then put it in her conference basket. The children were told that they were free to read their drafts to someone else before putting them in her basket; they were encouraged to do this, actually.

Now, during writing time, Dorothy calls the children up one by one based on whose folder is on the bottom of the pile in her conference basket. The youngster comes up and, after numbering each page in front of Dorothy, reads the draft out loud. If the youngster wants to publish, Dorothy writes down the child's words on a piece of newsprint exactly as the child reads them, carefully numbering the written lines (which, on a child's draft, are written with invented spelling). Dorothy's numbers match the child's draft pages. For example, if a child reads Dorothy two sentences that happen to be located on page one of the draft, Dorothy writes them *both* down beside the numeral one on the newsprint. The child continues and reads Dorothy page two, whereupon Dorothy writes down these words after the number two. After reading the whole draft to Dorothy, the child and Dorothy talk about the piece together. After telling the child how the draft makes her feel (e.g., excited, scared, happy), Dorothy asks questions like: Can I help you at all with your draft? Do you want to add anything else? Or Dorothy might ask the youngster about the pictures. Sometimes Dorothy wants more information, so she asks the youngster to elaborate.

Dorothy says that young children usually are willing to tell her much more about their topics than they are willing to write. She doesn't care that all the additional information they share doesn't get into their pictures or print because she knows their writing and drawing will catch up with their thinking later on. Occasionally Dorothy captures an important line from the child's dialogue and repeats it back to the youngster. If the child is so inclined, adding on becomes an option.

Now the child has two things in the manila folder: an original draft and Dorothy's written version. If the child wants the draft to be published for everyone to read, the youngster gets the appropriate number of sheets of publishing paper (the publishing paper, remember, is twice the size of the draft paper) and recopies the draft using Dorothy's written version. The child copies line by line, watching all spelling, spacing, capitalization, etc. When this has been completed, the youngster puts everything (the original draft, Dorothy's version, the corrected copy) back in the manila folder and puts the folder in Dorothy's publishing basket. When Dorothy has time, she pastes each picture from the child's rough draft onto the appropriate recopied page and also glues the child's invented spelling in the upper right hand corner. A published page is shown in Figure 1–30.

The final draft is then bound into an ever-growing anthology of the child's writing. Dorothy uses a binding machine that her school bought, which takes a plastic binding and hooks it onto a child's final draft by the pull of a lever. Quite often, the children operate the machine themselves.

Another Approach.   We're all different, so there's no one right way to publish. We know many first-grade teachers who don't worry a bit over publishing invented spelling. We've noticed that teachers who feel this way usually have very strong literature components in their classrooms. Many of them use basals only occasionally. Instead they use language experience at the beginning of the year (group and/or individual stories dictated by the students and read, copied, etc., by the children), and they use literature (whole books!) later on. They maintain that in this situation, with children seeing *lots* of print that utilizes conventional

FIGURE 1–30 A Published Page

spelling rather than invented spelling, children aren't harmed by reading the latter.

These teachers usually give their children draft booklets that look like small, thin books (white paper stapled to a piece of construction paper and folded over to look like a book). The children write during writing time, share and conference during conference time, and forget about formal publishing altogether. So be it. It's nice to see variation.

CONFERENCING TECHNIQUES

Conferences can be arranged between the teacher and children, between two children, or among small groups of children. We'll take a look at each type in turn.

Teacher-Child Conferences

Teacher-child conferences can be of two types: *individual*—one teacher, one child; or *teacher-group*—one teacher, a few children. Individual conferences can be *informal*, conducted during your writing time rounds, as we've mentioned earlier; or they can be *formal*, meaning prearranged. Drafts going through publication journeys are formal encounters, one-on-one interactions with authors during conference time.

During informal encounters (what we've called rounds), we find ourselves helping children trouble-shoot, usually by listening to problems, asking relevant questions, or making open-ended suggestions. For example, Randy, a second grader, might tell us he doesn't know how to end his piece. We might respond by suggesting that he read what he's written so far to a friend during conference time: Friends often help writers when they're stuck. If we have a child in mind who's great with endings, so much the better—we may suggest Randy conference with this writer. Alternatively, we may tell him what we do when we get stuck. For example, I often jot down ending alternatives and come back later to finish. ("Later" may be a few hours or a few days.)

Sometimes the problem is how to begin. If Michael, a first grader, tells us he doesn't know how to get started, we might ask him to show us his drawing (or cluster sheet), and then ask, "Michael, what do you think the kids are going to ask you when you share?" As he talks, we would encourage him to draw notes on his cluster sheet, or draw on his draft paper if he's chosen not to cluster.

Hopefully it's clear that informal conferences are short, the purpose being to help children move on quickly. Formal teacher-child conferences held with individual children are different: they've been planned and frequently center around a draft pulled from one of the conference boxes or folders.

During early, planned conferences over drafts pulled from Conference Box 1—conferences that center upon meaning rather than upon mechanical or grammatical issues—we often begin by telling the youngster how we felt about the piece as we heard (or read) it and by pointing to what we enjoyed the most. Then, we may attempt to help the youngster elaborate, often by inviting the child to talk about the topic.

During the early years, we generally ask for elaboration about things already brought up in the draft: "What else can you tell me about your bike?" "You say you go places on your bike. Where?" "You say it's blue; can you tell me more about that? A special sort of blue?" In first grade, much of this new information does not end up in the published version of the story, by the way. This may sound surprising, but we feel more comfortable with the notion that oral elaboration is enough with first graders. Their efforts to answer our questions need not be documented in black and white, although sometimes they are. At this level, what we hope we're doing when we ask children questions is modeling question-asking behavior, so typical of master writers. We *do* encourage older children, on the other hand, to add the information they think will make their draft either clearer or richer.

In order to help you help your children grow as writers, we have included Donald Murray's "Qualities of Good Writing" (see Figure 1–31), a list one of his students shared with us at a workshop we attended. This list will help you to identify what you most certainly know intuitively about good writing, but for which you may not have found good labels. We refer to this list all the time as we sort out what we might say to a child during our teacher-child conferences. Of course, like everything else in the teaching of writing, each situation is unique—no pat answers exist. The art of teaching writing lies in writing and reading yourself, and in being a sensitive human being. Take all the books you have on writing and put them on an old fashioned balance scale. On the other side put just three pieces of paper—one that says, "I write," another that says, "I read," and one more that says, "I am sensitive to this child's intention as well as his or her developmental level." Despite the lesser weight, this is the side of the scale that will weigh the most favorably in your continued attempt to be the best writing teacher you can.

FIGURE 1–31 Donald Murray's "Qualities of Good Writing"

1. **MEANING**
    There must be content in an effective piece of writing. It must all add up to something. This is the most important element in good writing, but although it must be listed first it is often discovered last through the process of writing.

2. **AUTHORITY**
    Good writing is filled with specific, accurate, honest information. The reader is persuaded through authoritative information that the writer knows the subject.

3. **VOICE**
    Good writing is marked by an individual voice. The writer's voice may be the most significant element in distinguishing memorable writing from good writing.

4. **DEVELOPMENT**
    The writer satisfies the reader's hunger for information. The beginning writer almost always overestimates the reader's hunger for language and underestimates the reader's hunger for information.

5. **DESIGN**
    A good piece of writing is elegant in the mathematical sense. It has form, structure, order, focus, coherence. It gives the reader a sense of completeness.

6. **CLARITY**
    Good writing is marked by a simplicity that is appropriate to the subject. The writer has searched for and found the right word, the effective verb, the clarifying phrase. The writer has removed the writer so that the reader sees through the writer's style to the subject, which is clarified and simplified.

Figure 1–32 is another list, which has examples of questions we have asked children to help them grow as writers. Nested within our list you will find questions that relate to Murray's qualities. A note of caution, however, is in order: Try not to overdo it when helping a youngster improve his work. We hardly ever address more than one issue at a time, and frequently a piece is published that is short on most of these aspects, but long on at least one.

We said that teacher-child conferences can be individual or teacher-group. Sometimes it helps to have a number of children around you and available for talking when you're holding a conference with a child. The other children listen and make good suggestions. Alternatively, sometimes a draft is so terrific we want a number of children to hear our responses to the writer. We choose to share our enthusiasm with a small group, rather than with the whole class at this point, because the draft is still in progress—but headed toward publication—and we want the author to feel the full impact of sharing in the author's chair later on. For these two reasons, we hold group conferences often.

To enable teacher-group conferences to happen easily, we usually ask the four or five children with whom we've planned a

FIGURE 1–32 Conference Questions Teachers May Consider

Introductory Questions

Tell me about your piece of writing.
Why did you choose this subject to write about?
What surprises you most about this draft?
What kinds of changes have you made from your last draft?
What problems did you have or are you having?
What questions did your conference partner have of you?
Where is this piece of writing taking you?
What questions do you have of me?

Questions That Deal with Meaning

Do you have more than one story here?
Underline the part that tells what this draft is about.
What is the most important thing you are trying to say here?
Explain how your title fits your draft.

Questions That Deal with Authority

Can you tell me more about this?
This part isn't clear to me. Can you tell me what you mean?
Can you describe this for me?

Questions That Deal with Voice

How does this draft sound when you read it out loud?
Circle the part that is most exciting.
Show me a place where I can tell that *you* have written this piece.

Questions That Deal with Development

Can you tell me more about it?
Do you have enough information?
Can you tell me where you are going in your draft?
How did you get to this place in your draft?

Questions That Deal with Design

Are you happy with your beginning and ending?
How does the beginning of your piece grab your reader's attention?
How have you tied your ending to your beginning?

Questions That Deal with Clarity

Can you be more specific here? (e.g., How did you go into the house?)
What are your action words? Can you add others?
Can you think of a different way to say this?
Is this the best word here?

Questions (When a Draft Is Not Finished) That Help a Writer Move On

What do you intend to do now?
What do you think you can do to make this draft better?
What works so well you'd like to try and develop it further?

Questions That Help Children See Their Growth As Writers

What did you learn from this piece of writing?
How does this piece compare to others you have written? Why?
Can you think of something new you tried in this draft that you have never
    tried before?
How are you a better writer now than you were at the beginning of the year?

conference to come to the conference table during conference time. They bring their writing folders and work on current drafts while we quietly talk with one youngster at a time. If we want the other children to join in, we ask them to put their pencils down and listen to the draft at hand. I thought Rebecca, a fourth grader from Sharon Kalinowski's class, might benefit from a group of children hearing her draft.

My Dad

Me and my dad play together. We play football and
baseball and we play basketball. He love me and my
sister and my mom very much. He has a very good job. He
likes to wach baseball and football. He likes to go to bed
all the time. He is very good to me. and he takes me
places like to the store like Hosin and Greens and kmarts.
My Dad is the best dad.

In general the children commented that Rebecca was lucky to have such a dad. Many of the other children live with only one parent. Also, they liked hearing he had a good job. Actually Rebecca's line about her dad's work prompted the question: "What does your dad do?" Rebecca wanted to tell, so she wrote, "He workes in a shop where cars are made." Well, that line perked more interest: "What exactly does he do?" Rebecca told us that she'd go home and ask, which she did. The point here is that the children were responding to Rebecca honestly, just like our first graders responded honestly to Christen's draft about cooking.

The same day I asked Rebecca to share her draft, I asked Brandon to share his. What a prize piece, I thought as I read it the night before. It's clear that Brandon knows when he has a good topic, and I wanted to share that with some children. See what you think.

Wrong Mom

Once in K-Mart I said, "Mom I'm going to the
toy isle." "Okay" she said, "I'll be looking in the
curtain place." "Okay" I said and off I went to
the toys. I looked at the Lego's. (I want this one
I thought.) until I walked to the next isle and
there she was (this isn't the curtain place.) Mom
can I buy this? Then She turned around and
looked at me. that isn't mom its someone else.
I was so embarrassed! I was so embarrassed I
started running around looking for my mom. I
found her and said come on lets buy this and get
out of here. finaly, we left and I was very glad!

Everyone was all over Brandon right away. What a topic! Brandon was all smiles, as I'm sure you'd be. Of course the children began to share their embarrassing moments, and before we knew it conference time was over. Too bad, because we could have talked forever. As the children were leaving the table, I pulled a book with dialogue from a nearby shelf. "Brandon," I said, "look at how authors punctuate conversation. This will help you prepare your draft for publication."

Peer Conferences

Children need time to talk to one another about their drafts, and not just about work that is headed for publication. They get stuck. They get tired of writing. They get bored with their own ideas. They need inspiration. All good reasons, we think, for letting them talk to one another, which they do during conference time.

As we've mentioned several times, modeling is important. Our all-classroom share time, from the beginning of the year, has been our model for peer conferences. When we sense that the children have grasped how to respond to a draft in the spirit of collegiality, we introduce peer conferencing. A few guideposts: 1) We like children to sign up for peer conferences so we can think about the pairs and make sure we approve (e.g., Will these two get anything done?). 2) We insist on not being disturbed during conference time, because we're busy too. 3) If children are in a peer conference, we ask them to log it in their writing logs (see the section entitled "The Manual"); we may ask them to tell us what they accomplished later on.

Sometimes children can hold small-group conferences, which are like extended peer conferences. When a number of children would like to conference together, all sharing their drafts and getting feedback from one another, we let them do so. We ask them to follow their conference guidelines and not to leave the group until everyone has had a chance to read. To insure this, we keep oaktag cards in the writing center labeled Group A, B, C, etc. and numbered sequentially. We pass one card out to each child in the group (e.g., A1, A2, A3, A4), and the children keep them in their folders until everyone has had a chance to read. If conference time is over before everyone has had a turn, the children keep the cards and meet with their group during the next conference period.

During the first few months of the school year, we're not sure how much gets done during peer conferences, whether two or twenty-two are involved. As the year progresses, however, the children get better, both in terms of their behavior and in terms of the quality of their interaction. Perhaps seeing their books published, their pieces appearing in classroom anthologies, hearing their work over the public address system during an all-school "spotlight on the author" radio show, perhaps these things make a difference. Or perhaps it's their teacher's honest commitment to literacy, his or her undying desire to hook children on language so that they love it, gregariously use it, remain unafraid of it, and seek to understand how and why it works.

All-Class and Small-Group Encounters: Focused Lessons

A lot of one-to-one teaching goes on in process classrooms, but it can't all be this way! Sometimes it's advantageous (and life-saving) to teach a concept to everyone or to a small group. All-classroom or small-group lessons can be oriented toward meaning or editing concerns; the procedure is the same for both. (We will give you the general procedure here, but see Section 2 for detailed lessons.) When they are very short, we call them mini-lessons. When we know they'll take up a whole period, we call them focused lessons.

First, identify an issue in a draft (e.g., sequencing, endings, conventions for writing dialogue, the use of semicolons). Ask the author if you can reproduce the draft on an overhead transparency. Make a ditto of it, if you can, and pass out red pencils with the copies. If you'd prefer not using a child's draft, make up one highlighting the issue and use this instead.

We discuss the issue with the class first. For example, in the piece about fish (see Figure 1–33), the concept we were to address was sentence order. We mixed up a paragraph from the basal reader first, then asked the children what was wrong. Later, we talked about how writers might get themselves into this fix. We noted that writing is difficult and demands attention, and that sometimes it is worthwhile just to get the whole draft out first, worrying about other things later: Drafts are just that, drafts.

Our next step is to put the draft we have prepared on the overhead and pass out the copies. Each child tries to make the piece better by himself, then pairs meet and work together. While working with the fish example, one child suggested we cut the transparency apart, by sentences. The children then took turns coming to the overhead, rearranging the sentences, and explaining their improvements. Talking about forming paragraphs was a natural outflow of this exercise, as was pronoun comprehension

My fish have little mouths but they eat like pigs but thats ok. **1**

I feed them every morning just a pinch. **2**

I started out with five fish 3 femails and 2 mails. **3**

Now I have 8 fish. **4**

And I like them a lot to. **5**

It's hard to hold the food in two fingers but I can do it. **6**

They are gupies. **7**

We did not name them yet. **8**

The cup we put the food in is about two inches long. **9**

I have pebbels that are colored and plants to in it. **10**

FIGURE 1–33 Fish Draft

(the "it" in sentence 10?). Correcting the spelling was also fun, but this came last (what a switch!).

PUBLISHING POSSIBILITIES: INDIVIDUAL BOOKS AND BEYOND

The list of publishing possibilities is endless. Of course, books are a favorite; we like to keep them simple. Since parent-teacher organizations are eager to know how best to spend their hard-earned money, we suggest binding machines (available in all office supply stores and costing about $300). Once a book is typed (or handwritten) and illustrated, and a cover is made, the binding process takes less than a minute.

Classroom literary journals are another option, and they can be sophisticated or kept simple. Simple ones entail children copying their drafts onto dittos (this would occur at the end of the publishing journey and replaces the bookmaking scenario), and teachers, or aides, running them off. Children can do the collating and stapling, and love to do so. Since literary journals can be sold, advertising proves to be yet another writing outlet.

As we've said, literary journals can be sophisticated as well. Berkshire Middle School in Birmingham, Michigan, wanted a professional look, so they had a local printer do theirs. Such journals get paid for through pledge campaigns, bake sales, or incentive grants offered frequently nowadays.

Classroom newspapers are also a natural outlet for children's writing. Children often write about trips and visitors, so why not use these drafts in your paper? A literary corner might become a permanent column, along with traditional news and editorial slots. Feature articles certainly could come from your children's writing.

National magazines such as *Stone Soup*, *Highlights*, and *Cricket* encourage children to write and to send in their work. Figure 1–34 is a list of magazines that publish children's work.

There are many ways to publish student writing in the classroom. Figure 1–35 (pages 58–59) is a list of forty-three innovative suggestions from teachers in the metropolitan Detroit area.

EVALUATION

Grades One and Two

It is hard writing about evaluation without getting philosophical. After reading a text written by Marjorie, a seven-year-old first grader, you can see that giving this piece a grade would not be easy.

I have to
atmit that I
wot get a sicker [sticker]

on my unit. Because it
was hard.
And I don't
whnat tu be a

scardy cat.
so I will tell
ya that I am not
a scardy cat.

FIGURE 1–34 Magazines That Publish Children's Work

Highlights for Children, Inc.
803 Church Street
Honesdale, PA 18431
(poems, stories, art, riddles, jokes, ages 3–12)

Stone Soup
P.O. Box 83
Santa Cruz, CA 95063
(poetry, fiction, plays, art, photos, ages 5–13)

Cricket Magazine
Box 100
La Salle, IL 61301
(poems, drawings, stories according to Contest Rules, ages 6–13)

Turtle
P.O. Box 567
1100 Waterway Blvd.
Indianapolis, IN 46206
(artwork only, ages 2–5)

Children's Playmate
Address same as Turtle
(poems, art, jokes, riddles, ages 5–7)

Prism
1040 Bayview Drive
Suite 223
Fort Lauderdale, FL 33304
(poetry, fiction, nonfiction, photographs, art, ages 5 and up)

The National P.T.A.
Reflections Contest
700 North Rush St.
Chicago, IL 60611
(poetry, prose, drama, art, music)

Raintree's Pub-A-Book
330 East Kilbourn Ave.
Milwaukee, Wisc. 53202

Shoe Tree
Sheila Cowing, Editor
215 Valley del Sol Drive
Santa Fe, NM 87501

Humpty Dumpty
P.O. Box 567
1100 Waterway Blvd.
Indianapolis, IN 46206
(artwork only, ages 4–6)

Childlife
Address same as Turtle
(art, stories, articles, book reviews up to 500 words, jokes, riddles, ages 7–9)

Childrens Digest
Address same as Turtle
(fiction, nonfiction, poetry—up to 700 words, favorite jokes, riddles, ages 8–10)

What will our grade reflect? Our ability as teachers? Marjorie's prior knowledge? Her product in light of other products written by children her age? The piece's meaning? Grammatical and mechanical correctness? Spelling correctness? Marjorie's effort? How much she has grown since her last effort?

From our point of view, we want to provide children with the type of evaluation and feedback that will produce skillful writers. For us, this means we must evaluate and give feedback throughout the writing process. Carol Steele, a writing consultant from Grand Rapids, Michigan, says (1986), "Evaluation needs to happen at the point in the process when the input will be most helpful." So when children stare at their empty topic sheets, we *help* them think of interesting aspects of their lives; we *read* first drafts and *point out* what has been said well; we *ask* for clarification when we feel lost as readers; we *look* for closure in pieces that lack endings; we *evaluate* and then *teach* the skills that need to be learned. The list could go on.

FIGURE 1–35 Ways to Publish Student Writing

1. Response to writing contests found in children's magazines such as *Cricket* or *Ranger Rick*

2. Classroom poetry corners

3. Classroom newspapers, fairly simple nowadays because of easy-to-use computer programs that set columns and incorporate drawings

4. School newspapers that include original student writing

5. Bulletin boards that highlight an author of the week

6. Bulletin boards that demonstrate the writing process—from first draft, through all revisions, to final product

7. Bulletin boards on selected topics

8. Books—both individual and class

9. Classroom literary journals

10. Grade-level literary journals

11. All-school literary journals

12. Program notes for class or school productions

13. Plays—written and produced by the children

14. Puppet shows—written and produced by the children

15. Research reports destined for a classroom book on a topic under study

16. Books on selected topics that go to waiting rooms in the community

17. Books written by older children for younger children

18. Radio shows on selected topics transmitted through the school's loudspeaker: sports broadcasts, author of the week, etc.

19. Student anthologies of their best writing over the school year

20. Letters to: authors, important public figures, people of interest to the class (e.g., local newspaper editors), thank-you notes, letters of inquiry, etc.

21. Student magazines: fashion, cars, computer information, etc.

22. Student tip sheets: tips on computer programs, school rules, dress code, lunchroom behavior, interesting and/or unusual games (e.g., ones that only require chalk, for example)

23. Instruction manuals ("how-to" books)

24. Signs for political campaigns, lemonade stands, school bake sales

25. Advertisements for used toys, old clothes, homeless puppies, etc.

26. Computer programs, with manuals, originated by the children

27. Game rules

28. Cookbooks

29. Cards: holiday, get-well, congratulations, birthday, unbirthday, etc.

30. Song lyrics

31. Author's page for original books

32. Notes sent to parents about class trips—before *and* after

33. Classroom sayings, proverbs, jokes, etc.

34. Chain novels—class or school-based

35. End-of-the-year "send-off" letters to school friends

36. Classroom door covers (poems, sayings, chants, rules of conduct, etc.)
37. Author's Chair—sayings, cheers, etc. (to be pasted on)
38. Classroom dictionaries
39. Make-believe products that require written language (e.g., cereal boxes, toothpaste tubes, boxed soup [directions needed], etc.)
40. Yearbooks
41. Documented picture albums from class trips or about class projects
42. Travel brochures written after a special trip
43. School handbooks

FIGURE 1–35 *(continued)*

By providing checklists and sets of questions we teach self-evaluation too. As Steele (1986) says, "Self-evaluation helps train students to turn their powers of observation and analysis toward their work." Through focused lessons, small-group conferences, teacher-child conferences, and peer conferences, children become increasingly adept at analyzing their writing. While we might consider evaluating their growing awareness of their writing needs or weaknesses, one quickly sees that the amount of teacher-child interaction is a crucial element in the equation. So we are back to square one, at least in terms of giving Marjorie's piece a grade.

If we have to give grades for writing, evaluating Marjorie on her performance in class seems a bit more realistic than assessing the quality of her drafts. Does Marjorie write during writing time? Does she listen when other children read their work? Is she growing in her willingness to write new and difficult words? These are all questions regarding her performance. But before evaluating Marjorie, even upon her performance instead of her products, we had better evaluate ourselves. Here is a list of teachers' behaviors that we routinely use to evaluate our *own* performance. It is our belief that if we do well in all of these areas, Marjorie will do well also.

As a teacher, do I

1. insist upon writing during writing time in order to grow as a writer?
2. share my own evolving drafts with the class?
3. keep track of children's progress in a systematic way?
4. have a structure or system in the classroom to support the writing period?
5. provide opportunities for children to publish in a variety of forms?
6. see to it that children share their work with other children?
7. seek out support materials to help children write?

8. have a literature component in my writing program?
9. share professional material with other teachers?
10. when holding teacher-child conferences, stay sensitive to the child's intention as well as his or her development level?
11. periodically show students how they are growing as writers?

What follows is a list of questions, a process checklist, that can help you evaluate each child's progress. Does this child:

1. _____ write during designated time?
   always   sometimes   rarely

2. _____ use constructive strategies for getting drafts started?
   always   sometimes   rarely

3. _____ take the conference period seriously?
   a) Is willing to help classmates by listening to their drafts
   b) Realizes other children may have meaningful suggestions
   always   sometimes   rarely

4. _____ show growth in his or her understanding of the difference between revising (e.g., adding on) and editing?
   quite a bit   some   very little

5. _____ use the support systems in the classroom (e.g., manual guidelines, spelling sheets, dictionaries)?
   frequently   occasionally   infrequently

6. _____ view revision as part of a healthy writing process?
   yes   at times   no

7. _____ actively participate during share time?
   almost always   on occasion   almost never

We don't mean to be glib by avoiding product evaluation, but at this point in time we simply don't know how, nor do we see any purpose in doing so. Instead we encourage you to press for performance evaluation during the early years. Let your report card reflect your knowledge of how children grow as writers by including a process evaluation, rather than a grade reflecting the quality of children's written work. Regarding Marjorie, by sharing our interpretation of her writing behavior with her, we feel we may help her products indirectly. For example, if she isn't using support systems, we can show her how; if she seems to be playing around during conference time, we can let her know *we* know, and that this matters. Some children benefit by knowing their behavior is being chronicled, and difficult as it is to admit this, we do believe it to be true. Therefore, we encourage periodic process evaluation. Like everything else we have written in this section, however, our checklist is by no means the end all. Some of the teachers we've worked with use only numbers 1, 3, 5, and 7. Others have asked their students to construct a list suitable for their classrooms, which may change as often as every marking period. The point is, our checklist is a prototype meant to be altered.

Grades Three Through Six

While we choose to center upon process evaluation when children are in first and second grade, it seems reasonable to begin evaluating children's products by third grade with the intent of giving feedback to parents in the form of commentary. By this age, and even earlier in some cases, children are leaving simpler forms behind (knowledge-based inventories, for example), in search of other forms. As readers, teachers interact with early attempts at story, or lengthy personal narrative, or even essay, at all levels—from issues that relate to meaning as well as to mechanics. To some extent, the qualities of good writing, such as design, development, and clarity, can be learned; and the mechanics of written language (e. g., grammatical preferences and conventional spelling) can be learned, too. Consequently, it seems wise to periodically take stock of how our children are doing.

A few teacher friends from the Walled Lake Consolidated School District and I have come up with an interesting possibility, one we would like to share.

In Walled Lake, the teachers at one elementary school, Oakley Park, are considering writing up a description of their students' writing development at each *grade* level. Right now some of the teachers are doing this individually for their own classrooms. That is, the descriptions have not become a grade-level enterprise, which might be the best way to go. Regardless, the descriptions will contain typical content characteristics, product appearance, developmental errors, and a depiction of typical, grade-level writing processes. The teachers involved believe that after writing up a class overview, it will become possible to think about each youngster in light of it and share these interpretations during individual parent-teacher conferences. These teachers are of the opinion that evaluation of a given child's cumulative products and processes will become a relative issue; that is, the teacher approaches parent conferences in light of the class (perhaps grade later on) overview: Here is where your child's written work and writing habits stand in relation to the rest of the class (or grade).

Below is Julie Janosz's description of her third-grade class's writing, along with a fictitious, but likely, scenario of an endeavor to use the description while talking with a parent.

CLASS DESCRIPTION

Content (e.g., topics, forms, use of detail, length, sentence structure)

1. Children like to choose their own topics in my room. They write about things that are close to them: family members, Mom, Dad, Aunt, Grandma; pets, loss of cats and dogs, a recent trip up north, amusement park, ball game; or special events in their lives, baseball tryouts, holidays. Pieces rarely lack meaning.
2. They include a profusion of details, which lends authority to their work.
3. Pieces usually do not extend beyond two or three double-spaced, handwritten pages.
4. Most sentences are declarative with some exclamations. There are few questions or commands.
5. Use of dialogue is minimal at first, but more eager writers begin to add some conversations by mid-year. In other words, most early drafts are almost totally narrative.

Appearance (e.g., draft states, use of illustration, recurring phenomena)

1. First drafts are usually messy.
2. Proofreading marks are rare at first.
3. Finished drafts are almost always illustrated—often a team effort and usually very detailed.
4. The proverbial "The End" will appear on most drafts.

Developmental Errors (areas in which children's work is under- (or over-) developed, where the intended form is not realized, or where there are typical grammatical, mechanical, or spelling errors)

1. Drafts contain lots of misspellings and mechanical errors; sometimes an entire draft has only one or two periods.
2. There are usually no paragraphs in first drafts.
3. Most sentences are short and usually simple—sentence patterns don't vary.
4. "And" is often used in place of periods.
5. The children tend to tell rather than show with the use of expressions such as "I like," or "It was fun."
6. Some drafts have so much detail the reader gets lost.
7. Sequence is a familiar revision issue. It seems they need to get all their information out first, then they can think about sequence (unless they've written a "breakfast to bed" account of a trip or experience).

**Process (what is going on in the room
during the writing period)**

Rehearsal. Third graders like to rehearse with a friend. Sometimes they do this before they begin their written rehearsal (e.g., cluster sheets, lists, drawing, library searches, interviews).

Drafting. Third graders are eager writers. They usually wait until a piece is completed before they share. Later in the year they will share parts of drafts. Though misspellings occur while drafting, third graders stay comfortably close to known vocabulary. They don't like to invent spellings of words they are not sure of.

Revision. Third graders revise orally with ease. At the beginning of the year, making additions, deleting information, or changing sentence order *in their written work* is another story—they find it difficult and often don't wish to do it. This behavior changes during the year as we "read like writers" (i.e., as we discuss parts of stories, essays, and poems as if we were the author), and as I give mini-lessons depicting strategies authors (both adult and child) use to improve their work.

Likely scenario with a parent:

Most of the children in my room like to choose their own topics. Michael does too. He usually writes about baseball, either about his team, how you help him at home, or about his baseball card collection. He's become the class expert. Like the other children, Mike loves minute details. He'll even include the type of pop he drinks while he waits his turn to bat. Most of his work is narrative—he tells everyone what's going on. He's not into using dialogue much. Since many of my children resist writing dialogue, I'm going to teach a mini-lesson on writing it soon. Michael's first drafts are never messy. It almost seems as though he's afraid to let his paper look out of control. I'm trying to encourage him to relax a bit; his first draft doesn't really need to look like a published piece. Also, he tends to use only words he knows how to spell. I'd like him to learn how to take spelling risks. You might help him at home by asking him to spell words he doesn't know how to spell and then congratulating him on how many of the letters appear in the conventional spelling of the word. All in all, Mike really works during writing time. He writes, offers to be a conference partner frequently, and listens when the other children share their work. During the rest of the year, I think you'll see improvement in his ability to proofread his work himself. Right now he depends on me to do a lot of this for him. Don't worry about his frequent choice of baseball as a topic. When children are learning to write, they need to care about their work and they need to make social connections with the class. As I've said, Mike's become our resident expert on baseball, and his self-concept is important to his growth as a writer.

Just as with the younger children, a *process* checklist such as the one we showed you earlier will appear on the report card in Walled Lake. If a grade *must* be given on your report card, you might consider averaging the scores from the process checklist by giving the best choice an "A," the next best choice a "B," and the lowest choice a "C" for each of the seven (give or take whatever you will) items.

Conclusion

What we have described in this section is a support system for the process of writing, which can be used with some variations throughout elementary school. For the sake of clarity, we have focused on the procedures that a teacher needs to follow to initiate and set up a process-writing classroom—topic choice, expanding a topic, peer conferences, revisions, teacher conferences, editing, and so on—at the risk of making the school day seem rather mechanical. Although it may take some time for both children and teacher to get used to these procedures, in our experience they do provide children with a sense of security and control, thus encouraging creative and productive work. Knowing the procedural ropes doesn't suppress the excitement children get from their writing; it channels it and keeps it alive.

REFERENCES

Blume, Judy. 1985. *The pain and the great one.* New York: Dell Publishing Co.

Calkins, Lucy McCormick. 1986. *The art of teaching writing.* Portsmouth, NH: Heinemann.

Elbow, Peter. 1973. *Writing without teachers.* New York: Oxford University Press.

Graves, Donald H. 1983. *Writing: Teachers and children at work.* Portsmouth, NH: Heinemann.

Graves, Donald, and Jane Hansen. 1983. The author's chair. *Language Arts* 60: 176–183.

Hemingway, Ernest. 1935. *Green hills of Africa.* New York: Charles Scribner's Sons.

Johnson, Tony. 1987. *The whale song.* New York: G. P. Putnam's Sons.

Murray, Donald M. 1980. How writing finds its own meaning. *Eight approaches to teaching composition.* Ed. Timothy R. Donovan and Ben W. McClelland. Urbana, IL: NCTE.

Romano, Tom. 1987. *Clearing the way: Working with teenage writers.* Portsmouth, NH: Heinemann.

Steele, Carol. 1986. Evaluation of writing. *Michigan Council of Teachers of English Newsletter* 38: 11–12.

Viorst, Judith. 1988. *The good-bye book.* New York: Atheneum.

Vygotsky, L. S. 1980. *Mind in society.* Cambridge, MA: Harvard University Press.

Yolan, Jane. 1987. *Owl moon.* New York: Philomel Books.

FOCUSED LESSONS

Introduction
Charles Temple

A decade ago in a book called *Writing, Reading, and Language Growth*, a teacher friend of ours, Ron Cramer, put forth what struck us at the time as a good idea that would help children write better. He would ask a volunteer to give him a paper that would be discussed by the whole class, and he would make an overhead transparency of the paper and project it for all to see (Cramer, 1978). In the discussion that followed, he would ask the students to point to parts of the paper that they especially liked —anything that struck them as interesting or well done. He often introduced terms for the qualities the students seemed to be responding to: "interesting detail," "exciting beginning," and so forth, and listed these terms on the blackboard, next to the screen. After the children had pointed to several good parts, Cramer would ask the children to point to parts of the paper that could be made better. As each student thought of something to be improved, he would challenge that child to decide *how* it could be improved. He introduced terms for those qualities, too, and made a list of them so that the students had named three or four qualities. Then he would lead the students to choose one quality from the list of potential improvements, discuss it briefly until he was sure every student understood the point, and finish by asking the students to get out papers of their own and see if they could improve them in the way that had just been discussed.

Our understanding about ways to teach children to write has changed much since Ron Cramer put forward this method; in fact, you can tell where you have come in your beliefs about teaching writing by examining your attitudes toward this method. For example, at the time it was proposed, the method seemed revolutionary, because it trusted so much in the children's own judgments as to what was good and bad in a piece of writing, and because it put children in the position of making critical judgments about each others' papers. But a few years after Cramer put forth his modest technique, writing teachers were thinking about the process approach to the teaching of writing, and Cramer's technique was pushed aside—perhaps because it was thought to be too conservative, too teacher centered. Now that we are several years into the process approach to teaching writing, we are able to find appropriate times for teaching both through individual counseling and through the type of group demonstration Ron Cramer proposed years ago. The technique for holding conferences with individual children, and leaving the initiative in their hands, was motivated by the sensible idea that the writer, and not the teacher, should be the authority when it came to her own paper. A child's sense of authority in the face of a teacher is a fragile thing that the teacher must work deliberately to nurture. But there are many things about writing that children don't know—and to leave all of these things to emerge in a conference seems wrong-headed, for at least three reasons. First, it will take a long time to get around to every technique or skill in writing we might want to pass on to a particular child if we try to do everything in conferences—especially since we want to reserve most of the time for him to talk about his paper and what he wants it to say. Second, we will end up repeating ourselves many times because, in truth, the set of techniques and skills any of us knows how to impart to a budding writer is shorter than we would like to admit. Third, to wait for the conference to tell a child something that she hadn't been told before about writing so often ends up implying that the child *should have known*—though in fact we're raising the point for the first time. (How many of us have been surprised by the child who nods her head violently and says, "I know! I know!" when we are gently trying to share something that is clearly new to her?)

We have come to balance the concerns of maintaining the child's initiative and authority as a writer on the one hand with the efficiency of direct teaching on the other. We conceive of our time for writing instruction in two divisions. First, there is *writing workshop time*, regularly scheduled periods of at least forty minutes each, three or more days a week, during which children are free to write on their own topics, share these works in various stages with their peers and with the teacher, edit them, and occasionally go about the business of publishing them. Second, there is *teaching time*, shorter periods arranged once or more a week during which we demonstrate usually a single point about writing to a group of students. These periods are considered separate, though we encourage students to carry over what they learn in teaching time to their own writing. That is why we often put the teaching time right before the workshop time—students may want to try out what we've shown them right away. Also, during conferences with the students, we can now talk about elements in their papers in the terms that we've introduced in teaching time and have a hope they know what we are talking about. (The payoff comes when we overhear children using these terms when they are talking about *each other's* papers: "This is good, but I think you need a stronger *lead*—I can't tell at the beginning what you're going to say in your paper.")

But what do we do during the teaching time? After all, teachers have been supposedly teaching children to write for years and have too often succeeded only in convincing children that they can't write, or don't want to. We have settled on what we call the *focused lesson*, a lesson that can take many different forms, but usually has certain features.

FEATURES OF FOCUSED LESSONS

1. *They focus on a single issue.* A focused lesson might deal with opening sentences or endings; it might talk about organization, and show the students one approach to it, such as organization by sequence in time; or show students a form for arranging a poem.

We remember that there will be other days and other focused lessons, and resist the urge to cover everything in a single lesson. We want the students to be able to leave the session being able to say aloud what they learned, and for this reason, we consider our terms carefully before the lesson begins, so the students will know what words like "organization" and "lead" and "closing" mean.

2. *They are taught by children themselves, or conducted as collaborations of the teacher and the group.* Among the lessons that

follow, Ruth Nathan describes one that grew out of a conversation she was having with a child about a paper he'd written. They had both realized that the paper needed a tighter ending, and after the student wrote one for it, he was so pleased with the result that he agreed to demonstrate for the whole class how he went about finding a good ending for his paper. Frances Temple shares a lesson in which she set out to teach the children a form to use for shaping poetry—the cinquain (she has found many uses for this form, some of which you will see in Section 3). In this lesson she walked through the steps of writing a poem using this form, asking the students to contribute the words at each step.

The purpose in both types of presentation is to keep the students actively involved and to make sure that the lesson is couched in terms that make sense to all the children.

3. *The students work the lesson just learned into papers of their own.* After the boy in Ruth's class taught his lesson on endings, she asked the rest of the class to take out a draft of a work in progress and think about an ending along the lines just presented. After Frances and her group had collaborated to write a cinquain, she asked the students to write one of their own.

But the lessons didn't stop there. Ruth has since found many occasions to talk about endings when conferring with a child about a paper. And now she can start from the assumption that the child has a notion of what she is talking about. Frances has brought out the cinquain form many times, too—for example, when she wanted the children to write a brief description of an animal (as part of a science lesson) or a historical figure (as part of a history lesson).

POSSIBLE TOPICS FOR FOCUSED LESSONS

Where do ideas for focused lessons come from? How do we know which ones to do, when?

Ideas for focused lessons come from the teacher's understanding of how children learn to write. These ideas begin with whatever enables them to write a lot, to develop satisfaction, confidence, and fluency. Then, as the students appear ready, teachers go on to help them develop sophistication and refinement in their writing. What follows is a list of topics that we might use for focused lessons.

- *Choosing topics:* Where do we get topics to write about? How do we convert our personal experiences into material for writing? These are concerns every beginning writer has, and we do a series of demonstration lessons in this area.

- *Narrowing topics:* Suppose a child has chosen "dogs" as his topic—is he going to write *everything he knows* about dogs? How can he narrow his topic down so that he can write one hard-hitting page about it?
- *Beginnings:* Where do you start? How much introducing should you do before you get on to the interesting part? How do you get readers' attention right away? Beginnings, or leads, as journalists call them, deserve several lessons.
- *Endings:* How do you stop? What kind of thought do you want to leave the reader with?
- *Organization:* This covers many different challenges. What should go first? What next? What after that? There are different orders of material for descriptions, explanations, stories, and poems; and there are many lessons, and many individual conferences, that will be devoted to this topic.
- *Showing, not telling:* A child writes, "The dog was mean." The reader wants to know "How did he act, what did he do to make you say that he was mean?" The writer needs to learn not to pass on summary judgments, but rather to paint a picture with words that will let the reader see what the writer saw and draw her own conclusions.
- *Characterization:* When we read a story, we want to be able to visualize the characters, we want to get to know them. We also want to know what they are doing in the story: what role does each character play? Lessons on characterization will involve studying literature. They may also take the form of creative dramatics, as students role-play the way a certain character moves, talks, and feels as a warm-up for writing about the character.
- *Editing:* In this book we suggest having students compare each other's work to a list of editing points, including punctuation, capitalization, left out words, and the like. Each of these points is best introduced in a focused lesson.
- *And, for beginners:* Kindergarten and first-grade children should be encouraged to draw, scribble, and write with invented spelling—whatever they need to do in order first to get something to say and say it fluently and confidently. Later they will move on to refine their skill in writing. In the beginning, most children need to be shown a range of expressive choices open to them, and this is best done in focused lessons.
- *Invented spelling* deserves special lessons: both to encourage children to take advantage of their abilities to invent spellings

in order to express themselves and eventually to get them to move beyond invented spelling to standard spellings for individual sounds and for words.

Focused lessons can be introduced spontaneously, sparked by an issue that emerges in a teacher's conference with a single student. The teacher may find an issue in the student's paper—something she has done really well, or is glaringly in need of correcting—and may decide to go over the issue with the whole class. Ruth Nathan starts off this section with a focused lesson that began in just that way. Or the teacher may decide simply to introduce a lesson on, say, the organization of stories, when it occurs to him that the students are ready for a new challenge. Kathleen Juntunen and Frances Temple give us focused lessons that emerged this way.

A Focused Lesson on Descriptive Writing

Ruth Nathan

I develop focused lessons using my children's rough drafts. I frequently use focused lessons to begin our writing workshops, which we have at least three times a week.

First, I spot a strong but "wanting" draft. Then, with the author's permission, I type it and set it aside. During my first conference with the child I take notes, carefully. (This first teacher-child conference always deals with *meaning*.) Here is how I used this process recently for a focused lesson on descriptive writing.

The piece you're about to read, written by Paula, a fourth grader, is a fine example of fantasy. I say it is fine because Paula has 1) indeed, written a story; 2) used quite a bit of supporting detail, which lends authority to her piece; 3) used exaggeration effectively to build suspense and interest; and 4) let her voice ring through. (Most mechanical, grammatical, and spelling mistakes have been corrected so you can concentrate on meaning.)

Fishing

One sunny Monday morning in the summer I got up and said, "Today is a good day for fishing." So I got up, got dressed, and ate. I called my friend Christy. She is in fifth grade. She said her mom would let her. We got our stuff and we went to Wolverine Lake.

I put some bait on the hook. Christy caught 12 fish before I even got my bait on.

By the time I got my bait on, Christy caught 18 fish. Suddenly, when we were ready to leave, my bobber went down. I said, "Help Christy, I'm falling in." I reeled it in as fast as I could. Finally I got it. It was a whale!

We dragged it home. We had a fish fry. I had 10 pieces of fish. It was good. We went there to fish all the time.

My *meaning* conference with Paula opened by my asking her if I could help in any way. She said no, she liked the piece just as it was. I then went on, explaining specific reasons why I thought her story was well done (the reasons I've enumerated above). Later, I asked her a couple of questions about the "catch." I was trying, I said, to picture her on the pier with Christy—catching a whale! "What was the first thing you felt?" I asked.

"Nothing," was her reply.

"Well, how did you know you had hooked a fish?"

"I felt a tug," Paula said.

For the next five minutes, Paula and I talked about what she saw, felt, and heard as she brought the whale in. I took notes for her, since she is a reluctant writer and since time was becoming an issue, as well. This is exactly what she said:

I felt a tug. It started to pull me into the lake. I yelled for help. Christy pulled me and something gigantic came out of the water. We heard slapping from the fish opening and shutting its mouth. It was flapping around. His tail was going up and down. It was hard pulling him. My arms hurt and my hands were sweating.

I read Paula's words back to her and asked if she wanted to include this new information in her story. Since her own, colorful language pleased her, she eagerly said yes. Paula had to make a few changes to accommodate her new information; she did this on her own. Below is her revised story. (The new information is in italics.)

Fishing

One sunny Monday morning in the summer I got up and said, "Today is a good day for fishing." So I got up, got dressed, and ate. I called my friend Christy. She is in fifth grade. She said her mom would let her. We got our stuff and we went to Wolverine Lake.

I put some bait on the hook. Christy caught 12 fish before I even got my bait on.

By the time I got my bait on, Christy caught 18 fish. Suddenly, when we were ready to leave, my bobber went down *and I felt a tug. It started to pull me into the lake. I yelled for help. Christy pulled me and something gigantic came out of the water. We heard slapping from the fish opening and shutting its mouth. It was flapping around. His tail was going up and down. It was hard pulling him. My arms hurt and my hands were sweating.* Finally I got it. It was a whale!

We dragged it home. We had a fish fry. I had 10 pieces of fish. It was good. We went there to fish all the time.

A few days later I was ready to use Paula's draft for a focused lesson on descriptive writing. I gathered the children together on the benches we have in the front of the room. All of them brought a pencil, a copy of Paula's draft, and one of their own drafts. On

Paula's typed draft, the information she had added was printed in italics (as above), while the rest was printed in a standard font.

Paula did most of the talking from this point forward. She read her original draft and then read the new draft with her description of the catch. I spoke to the class about how important it is to pay attention to all our senses when we're trying to help readers picture a situation, and I explained how I questioned Paula about what she heard, saw, and felt as she and Christy landed the whale.

The class really got "into it," as the expression goes. They immediately turned to their own drafts and looked for places where they could add a descriptive touch. I asked them to put a little red dot where they had more to tell (Calkins, 1986). When they went back to their seats, I explained, they could revise.

In the meantime, the children had questions for Paula. For example, they wanted to know what it was Christy's mom would let her do: " 'She said her mom would let her,' " they read. "Let her what?"

Paula replied, "She let her go fishing."

At this point I made a suggestion: The children could ask Paula for clarification and Paula would put a red dot above these trouble spots. Then she could add what she wanted to add and not include information she felt was unnecessary. In other words, Paula was still in charge. Based on her classmates' questions, here is where Paula put dots:

One sunny Monday morning in the summer I got up and said, "Today is a good day for fishing." So I got up, got dressed, and ate. I called my friend Christy. She is in fifth grade. She said her mom would let her. We got our stuff and we went to Wolverine Lake.

I put some bait on the hook. Christy caught 12 fish before I even got my bait on.

By the time I got my bait on, Christy caught 18 fish. Suddenly, when we were ready to leave, my bobber went down *and I felt a tug. It started to pull me into the lake. I yelled for help again. Christy pulled me and something gigantic came out of the water. We heard slapping from the fish opening and shutting its mouth. It was flapping around. His tail was going up and down. It was hard pulling him. My arms hurt and my hands were sweating.* Finally I got it. It was a whale!

We dragged it home. We had a fish fry. I had 10 pieces of fish. It was good. We went there to fish all the time.

Now, here is Paula's piece as it stands today, which is illustrated and bound in book form for everyone to read. (I've put Paula's new information in bold italics for you, while the added, descriptive information about the catch remains in regular italics.)

Fishing

One sunny Monday morning in the summer I got up and said, "Today is a good day for fishing." So I got **out of bed**, got dressed, and ate **breakfast**. I called my friend Christy. She is in fifth grade. She said her mom would let her **go fishing**. We got our stuff and we went to Wolverine Lake.

I put some bait on the hook. Christy caught 12 **bluegill** before I even got my bait on.

By the time I got my **popcorn** on, Christy caught 18 fish. Suddenly, when we were ready to leave, my bobber went down *and I felt a tug. It started to pull me into the lake. I yelled for help again. Christy pulled me and something gigantic came out of the water. We heard slapping from the fish opening and shutting its mouth. It was flapping around. His tail was going up and down. It was hard pulling him. My arms hurt and my hands were sweating.* Finally I got it. It was a whale!

We dragged it home. **It was heavy to drag but we made it.** We had a fish fry. I had 10 pieces of fish. It was good. We went there to fish all the time.

By the way, Paula wanted an About the Author page. Here's what she wrote:

Paula [last name] was born in 1977. She now lives in Walled Lake, Michigan. Fishing is Paula's hobby. She goes fishing a lot with her dad also.

Things Are Not Always
What They Seem:
A Focused Lesson on Clarity
Kathleen Juntunen

Lions Game

It all started on a Wednesday around 6:00 when the phone rang. It was Scott. He invited me to a Lions pre-season game and to sleep over.

When the Saturday came I got my glasses. When I left for Scott's house I was very excited and I had 6 dollars and some rolls to give to Scott's mom and dad. When I got there Scott was watching a Star Trek show. (What episode? I don't know.)

When I read this first page of Owen's draft, several areas stood out as possibly being off the topic, so this was what I decided to concentrate on during my conference with him, which went like this:

"Owen, I like the lead in this piece; it makes me want to find out about the phone call." Owen nodded. "Tell me, what is your main purpose in writing this piece? What do you want to get across to the reader?"

"I want to tell about going to the Lions game and tell how much fun it was."

"I see. There are a couple of places that I'm not sure how they relate to your purpose, and I wondered if they were part of your topic. Would you please read your piece to yourself and underline any parts you think a reader might wonder about?" He underlined as shown above.

"That's very interesting because those are the very parts I had in mind. Let's start with the glasses. When you said you got your glasses, does that mean you went to some drawer and took them out, or does it mean they were new and you went to the store to pick them up?"

"They were new and I went to pick them up."

"I see. And were they important, then, for you to be able to see the game?"

"Yes, because before I got them, I couldn't see very well."

"Then this part is really not off the topic at all, but I as a reader wondered about it. What do you think you could do to make this part clear to the reader?"

"I need to tell more about getting them."

"I think that would be helpful."

"Now, what about these rolls? I'm not sure I know what kind of rolls they were. The first thing I thought of was those rolls of wrapped money and you were paying for the ticket with them."

"No, they were the kind you eat."

"Why were you taking them to Scott's mom and dad?"

"I'm not sure."

I waited as Owen thought for a few moments, then I asked, "Well, where did the rolls come from?"

"My mother made them . . . I guess she did that because I had done so many things with Scott, and now I was going to the game."

"Oh, were they like a courtesy, a thanks to his parents?"

"Yeah."

"Then that part is not really off the topic either."

"No."

"Could you make that part clearer?"

"Yes."

"What will you do?"

"I'll explain about the rolls."

"Let's look at the last part you underlined. Do you have any explanation that you left out here that might tie this in with the topic?" Owen thought for a few moments and answered, "No, I don't think it matters that Scott was watching television."

"Then you think this is not needed?" Owen nodded.

I am always on the lookout for children's pieces that can be used as class lessons to model the kinds of things my students need to consider in their writing. Since Owen's fourth-grade class was just beginning to familiarize themselves with the writing process, I thought this piece would lend itself to a simple and straightforward focused lesson on clarity and staying on the topic. So I said to Owen, "I think this would be great to use with the class. Would you be willing to conduct a lesson from the author's chair based on what we just did together?"

"What would I do?"

"Well, we can give each person a copy of your piece and you can read it to them and ask if there are any parts they don't understand. You can take it from there, doing what we just did together. I think it would be interesting to see if they find the same places we talked about. If they do, you can talk about the parts as you did with me, and if they don't, you can discuss whatever comes up. What do you think?"

"Okay."

The next writing period, we proceeded as planned. After the children had finished the underlining, Owen called on Mike to read the first portion he had a question about. Mike read, "When the Saturday game came, I got my glasses."

I asked the class how many people had underlined the same part. All nineteen members of the class raised their hands. Owen then told the class how he planned to clarify this portion. He next found eight students had selected the portion about the "6 dollars and some rolls." The student Owen called on wanted to know what kind of rolls they were, and he explained again. Owen was clearly enjoying his leadership role in this lesson.

Seventeen students had underlined the part about Scott watching television, and one had underlined just the part in parentheses about what episode. The lesson turned out to be almost a duplicate of the conference between Owen and me.

After we completed the lesson, I thanked Owen, and the class applauded his contribution. When I asked the students what they thought this lesson showed, they concluded it is important for an author to conference about his writing to find out if the reader understands what he is trying to communicate. I then commented, "Also, as I found with this piece, you can't jump to conclusions before you talk to the author. I thought some of these sentences were off the topic, but when I talked to Owen, he showed me they were not. As authors, we sometimes assume the reader knows more about the topic than we do, so we forget to put in important details. It's important to think about this when you reread your writing."

"Now I would like each of you to take out a draft you have finished or are working on and read it to see if there are any areas that are off the topic or that you think may be hard for the reader to understand. Please use your red pencil so we can compare what you changed or added with your original writing. Next time we have writing workshop, you can read your piece to someone to see if they think your writing is clear and on the topic."

Illustrating, or How to Draw a Wayward Horse

Kathleen Juntunen

Within a classroom there are usually a few children who believe they're good at drawing. Many, however, are more often disappointed than pleased with what they draw and often find illustrating a frustrating experience. Finding myself in the latter category, I have empathy with the students who struggle to illustrate their stories. So I decided to try this lesson to alleviate the "I can't draw" anxiety the children frequently express, beginning around third grade.

I begin by asking, "How many of you like to draw?" The majority of students raise their hands. "Do any of you have trouble sometimes?" Again the majority raise their hands. "What kinds of things are difficult for you to draw?"

The children's first response is invariably, "People."

"Is there anything else you find hard to draw?"

The second response is most often, "Animals."

"What can you do if you want to draw something like an elephant, let's say, and you are having difficulty?"

"Get a picture of an elephant to look at."

"Good. That can be very helpful. There are also some other things you can do when you are illustrating your writing that can make the job easier for you and fun for the reader. Today I am going to show you some things other students have drawn when they don't want to draw people or animals over and over [see Figure 2–1, a through f]. You can see these children thought of some unusual ways to illustrate their writing. They're interesting for the reader, too, because they are often unexpected."

After I show the illustrations and read the accompanying text, I say, "Now we're going to have some fun practicing. I have written four different situations that I am giving each of you to illustrate." After the papers are distributed, I say, "First we'll read these together."

1. Harry knew he shouldn't have eaten all that food. Now he was miserable and feeling sorry for himself. He felt like he

Crunch

After that we were walking along the street and horse carriages were trotting by. Then we saw the fort. The fort is a really big wall that is blocking all the houses at Mackinac Island during George Washington's days.

(a)

chomp! chomp!

So some people said, "Don't hold the reins so hard." So I didn't and Strawberry started to trot down the street. He started to go on the sidewalk and began eating grass.

(b)

When it was time for school, Connie's mother helped her put on her snowsuit. Mother helped Connie put on her boots. Then mother said, "Where are your mittens?"
Connie answered, "I don't know."

(c)

"I won't lose my mittens any more. I'll be real careful, I promise. I don't want mitten clips. Waaaa!"
"I'm not going to buy you more mittens. You'll wear the mitten clips."
"I don't want to!"
"I don't care if you want to or not. You're wearing the mitten clips."
"No."
"Yes."
"No. Waaaa!"

(d)

FIGURE 2–1 Different Ways to Illustrate Writing. (a)–(b) By Brandi Blaisdell. (c)–(f) By Norishige Abe.

(continued)

After supper, Connie's mother said, "I have a surprise for you." She handed Connie a brown bag. Connie opened the bag. In the bag was a brand new pair of mittens. Attached to the mittens were mitten clips.	Every day Connie wore her new mittens and mitten clips. She did not lose her mittens. She played in the snow every recess. She made snowmen with Mother. She made a snow horse with Dad. She had a good time playing in the snow.
(e)	(f)

FIGURE 2–1 *(continued)*

was about to burst. (Illustrate this without drawing a complete person.)

2. The stable man had rented Suzie a horse much too big for her to handle, but he said Silver was the only horse left. Suzie began to be sorry she had agreed to ride Silver because he kept going off the trail to eat the grass. He didn't know how to read the "Keep off the grass" sign! (Illustrate this without drawing a complete person or a complete horse.)

3. This is the most important game for the football team, and now there are only seconds left. The score is tied. It is up to Bob to make the field goal for a win. His stomach is jumping like popcorn as he stands in front of the ball. (Illustrate this without drawing complete people.)

4. Janet's hamsters had so many babies, her mother told her she had to sell them. So Saturday morning, Janet made a sign to put in front of her house. (Illustrate this without drawing a complete person or a complete hamster.)

After we read each situation and the directions, I continue, "Underneath each situation, make your drawing. You may draw *parts* of animals or people if you like. And remember, you may use writing as part of your picture. Discuss this with the people in your group if you wish, or work alone. I am going to be doing this activity with you. Let's see how inventive we can be with our drawings."

The students really have fun doing this and always come up with a variety of ideas. For the first situation, many students draw a large stomach and sometimes include the word "Groan" in the picture. This is a good time to talk about how thinking to oneself is depicted in cartoons. Some draw a table loaded with food; others show a great explosion.

For number two, most students incorporate a sign that reads "Keep off the grass." A few will draw portions of a horse's body.

In the third situation, many show a football flying through the air. This gives us a chance to discuss how an artist shows motion. Some students include just the goal posts and/or many circles to represent the heads of the crowd in the stands.

For the last scenario, many students include signs, "Hamsters, 50 cents each," and/or a hamster's cage. A few students show the mother-daughter exchange with conversation "clouds" as they had seen in Figure 2–1, d. The students enjoy sharing their completed work, and most will now try similar ideas in illustrating their own writing.

A Focused Lesson on Sequence of Ideas and Sentence Combining
Kathleen Juntunen

Mrs. Grey's third-grade class had just been shown how to generate their own topics and had written their first drafts. I was a writing consultant working in Mrs. Grey's class. Becky chose to write about Halloween:

I had 3 bags of candy. I had Whoppers, Snickers, bubblegum, Milk Duds, Money, Milky Way, Nerds, suckers, and Kit-Kats. I was a witch last year. I had green and black make-up. I had green fake nails. I had orange hair. I had a black dress. My friends were Patty and Becky. Patty was a Bum. Becky was a pumpkin. I was out till 9:30 P.M. I was out 2 hours. I went door to door Trick-or-Treating.

When Becky shared her draft with the class, the students told her they liked the details she had included: the names of the candy, the green and black make-up, the fake nails and orange hair. Then at the end of the period, while the other children were writing, I talked to Becky about her draft. I asked her to read it again and see if she thought the sentences were in the best possible order. Upon rereading, she immediately realized some of the sentences could be rearranged chronologically. I then asked her to number the sentences accordingly. When she finished, she gave me her permission to use the draft for a lesson on sentence order.

Before the focused lesson, I recopied and numbered each of her sentences (as she had originally written them) on an individual line with plenty of space between each line and then made ditto copies of it for the class. In addition, I made a transparency of the ditto, which I cut into the individual sentences for use with the overhead projector.

I began the lesson by saying, "Today we are going to spend a few minutes talking about sequence. Sequence means putting your thoughts in clear and logical order. Becky has agreed to allow us to use her writing for this lesson. You'll be working with a partner on this." Each pair of children was given two pairs of scissors, but just one copy of the paper. I read the sentences aloud and said, "You probably noticed some of these sentences seem out of order. You and your partner will share the task of cutting these sentences apart. After you discuss the order you think they should be in, rearrange the strips according to the way you have agreed."

After about ten minutes, I called on Becky to share her changed sentence order. As she read the sentence order by number, I projected the transparency strips to show the class:

3. I was a witch last year.
4. I had green and black make-up.
5. I had green fake nails.
6. I had orange hair.
7. I had a black dress.
8. My friends were Patty and Becky.
10. Becky was a pumpkin.
9. Patty was a Bum.
12. I was out 2 hours.
11. I was out till 9:30 P.M.
13. I went door to door Trick-or-Treating.
1. I had 3 bags full of candy.
2. I had Whoppers, Snickers, bubblegum, Milk Duds, Money, Milky Way, Nerds, suckers, and Kit-Kats.

A discussion ensued when the students suggested other possibilities. We talked about the idea that there were several ways to arrange the sentences that made sense and, as the author, Becky would decide what she wanted to do.

The previous sequence piece also proved to be a good example to usc for a lesson on combining sentences. For this lesson, I first composed this simple paragraph:

We bought a dog. We bought him at a pet store. He is brown. He is large. He has curly hair. We took him home. We gave him a bath. We bought him a rubber bone to play with. He likes to play ball. He likes to ride in the car. He is cute. We love him.

At the beginning of the lesson, I distributed a copy of the paragraph to each student. After we had read the piece and discussed how connectors can be used to combine sentences, we talked through how some of the sentences in this piece could be combined. I wrote the various suggestions on the overhead projector as the children talked. Here is the version we finally ended up with from our group effort (I explained that this was not the only possible version):

We bought a dog at a pet store. He is large. He has brown, curly hair. We took him home and gave him a bath. We bought him a rubber bone to play with. He likes to play ball and he likes to ride in the car. He is cute and we love him.

I then gave each student a copy of Becky's piece, as she had rearranged it, and, after breaking into pairs, I asked them to discuss with their partner the sentences that seemed to belong together and then circle them. The children had no difficulty in separating the sentences into four groups: about the candy, the description of the costume, the friends, and the time. They worked together and combined those sentences they thought needed combining. Then one person wrote the results the pair had agreed on. While the children were working, I circulated and distributed blank transparencies and pens. I asked each couple to copy their sentences on a transparency. After a few minutes, we shared and discussed the results with the whole class. Most of the children combined only the parts about Becky's costume and her friends. Here are two examples:

Last year I was a witch and I had black and green makeup, fake green nails, orange hair, and a black dress.

My friends were Patty and Becky. Patty was a bum and Becky was a pumpkin.

During the course of the year, I looked for other examples of student work to use for similar lessons to reinforce sequencing and sentence combining skills.

Invented Spelling: A Classroom Approach

Ruth Nathan

When children write before they begin formal schooling, they approach the task creatively—they have a great big puzzle to solve. Imagine, if you will, a precocious five year old writing on the side of his bathtub with soap-chalk. He wants to spell, "I love my boat." What does he write? Perhaps, "I lv Mi bt." Or, maybe, "Ilvmibot," or even, "pqstuvcoooo." Do his parents mind? Not really. Like learning how to talk, most parents celebrate initial messages, even if manufactured with invented spelling.

Kindergarten and first-grade teachers who encourage writing attempt to capitalize on children's creativity in their classrooms. Like parents, these teachers celebrate invented spelling because they know that as their children begin to read, their invented spellings will look more and more conventional.

We'd like to share how we begin writing with children in kindergarten and first grade. While it is true many youngsters come to school writing, not all do. We want to encourage those who haven't to give it a try.

Taking a developmental point of view, we begin with a writing center. During the school day, children in kindergarten may choose to go to the writing center, just as they may choose to go to the blocks. There's no push, but we deliberately make the center a very inviting choice. First graders usually visit the center as they wait for their classmates to arrive in the morning, as well as later in the day as opportunities arise.

We load the center with all sorts of paper (e.g., lined, unlined, index cards, old computer cards, discarded computer paper, coffee filters); pens of every color; pencils; erasers; scissors; letter and picture stamps; letter, number, and shape stencils; alphabet strips; picture piles; envelopes; dictionaries; chalk boards and chalk.

As we see writing attempts emerge (which at this point often consist of copying or stamping words and letters from books), we begin labeling characters from the stories we read. For example, on the day we read *Jack and the Beanstalk*, we draw Jack and the Giant on a portable blackboard and label all their limbs and parts. Likewise, we label the Gingerbread Man on another day, the Troll on another, all the Wild Things from Maurice Sendak's *Where the Wild Things Are* on another—you name it. We do this with the children, letting the children sound out as they go: "YLD HEGS" for "Wild Things," "MSTR" for "Monster," "TOL" for "troll." We even retell the stories ourselves and write them in invented spelling as the children help. "Wuns apon a tim tr was a ltl boe namd Max." We have fun.

Before we know it, invented spelling is occuring at the center. Whenever we see it, we celebrate the risk taken. When the time is right (usually about January in kindergarten, by late September in first grade), we do a spelling activity together, where all of the children give invented spelling a try. Because of what has gone on before, we have a very high success rate—often 100 percent. This is what we do:

First the children and their teacher gather in a circle and talk a little about the writing center and how we have all tried to write. The children eagerly share their feelings. "We love to send letters," they say, which they do via our classroom mailbox. Then we explain that we know an author who likes to label just like they do. We bring out all the Richard Scarry books we can find and pass them around. The children begin to guess what the words say. They team up, naturally, and "oooh" and "aaah" over how right their guesses are.

Next we surprise the children by giving them each a picture of a bear. We've Xeroxed our bear, leaving just a few lines (perhaps eight—all on his right side) pointing to parts of his body. We tell the children to go back to their seats with their papers and to watch for the bear on the wall. In the meantime, we've made a transparency that looks just like theirs and have now turned on the projector lamp. There's lots of excitement and noise at this point, which we encourage.

Each child has a pencil. We start at the top. "What's this?" we ask.

The children yell, "His ear."

"How shall we label *ear*? Eeear, eeear," we say.

A few yell out, "EEEEEE."

"Okay! Now, you try and finish it yourself. Write the letters you hear right on your bear." They do, eagerly. Then we say, "Who would like to share what they've written?" Hands fly up. Here are a few of the invented spellings for "ear" that we've gotten: "er," "eri," "eir," even (of course) "ear." Though "ear" is the "book spelling" (that's what we call conventional spelling), we just accept it as another invented spelling attempt.

Now we're in business. Next comes "head." "How shall we start it?"

"With an 'h,' " they yell.

"Okay! Now, finish it yourself." And they do. Typical spellings for head include: "heed," "head," "hiad," "had," and "haed." We continue for a little while longer and then stop. By this time we've labeled about four words; we'll finish the rest another day.

Before we stop, however, we play a spelling game. We pass out small chalkboards, familiar fare in most kindergarten and first-grade classrooms. We say, "Think of a word you don't know how to spell. Make it a real hard one. Now, write it on your chalkboard, but don't let anyone see—and don't tell anyone what you're writing." The children do this eagerly. Then, one by one, we call them up to the front of the room. The first child turns his board over so the whole class can see it. Now the children guess what this child has written. It's truly amazing how facile they become at reading one another's writing. If we're unsure, we ask the child to whisper the answer (that is, the word) in our ear. This way we can help the youngster give meaning clues—a cheater's version of twenty questions.

The next day we finish labeling our bear. From now on, we feel very secure handing out draft booklets and swinging into a full writing period.

A Focused Lesson on Endings

Ruth Nathan

Just like a good lead, a good ending can do any number of things to a text. It can wrap up a piece by summarizing it; it can be generative and create additional questions in the reader's mind; or it might add a philosophical touch by taking a reader beyond the literal interpretation of a text (e.g., by giving it a "this is life" perspective).

Children's personal narratives usually end with the last thing that happened in a sequence of events. Sometimes, not knowing exactly how to end their pieces but feeling as though they need to add something more, youngsters write dramatically (i.e., in capitals or multicolored splashes) "the end." Of course, the last thing that happened or multicolored splashes for endings are fine, but by third grade we like to share alternative possibilities. The piece you're about to read was written by Chris, a sixth grader. It's a first draft of the second and last chapter in his book, *Snowballing*. Typically, his first draft ends with the last thing that happened to him and his friends.

The Fun Just Begins

One day a couple of my friends and I went skiing. And when we got up the chair lift we took snowballs and one time we threw snowballs and hit some teenagers. They started chasing us. They caught Mike Willamson because he fell and broke his collar bone. But Piagentini and I were still going. We finally made it to the bottom and popped off our skies. Then we ran inside and hid under a table but that didn't do much good because they walked in and stood in front of our table. Then bent over and saw us. We thought we'd be dead. But it was my brothers so they just left. Then we went back to get Mike, but he wasn't there. The ski patrol must of picked him up already. We went to the ski patrol lounge and there he was. He was wearing a brace and would have to wear it for 5 months.

While this piece needed a lot of work, such as clarification, paragraph markers, and punctuation, I saw it as a good opportunity to talk about endings with Chris, as well as with the class later on. At our next teacher-child conference, I read him a few short pieces from *Ranger Rick*, a science magazine for younger children, pieces with different types of endings. We talked about the alternatives, and then Chris read his ending aloud to me. He didn't know what to do right away, but he felt he might do something. We began talking about the "this is life" perspective, and Chris suggested making a list outlining the good and bad aspects of "snowballing" other kids. Here is what he jotted down on a piece of scratch paper.

Good	**Bad**
It's fun	being afraid of
throwing	getting beat up
getting chased	
getting hit	

Chris's eyes lit up as he looked at this list. He went back to his seat and wrote, "Then we went home and started talking about snowballing. We were laughing about the whole thing. It's fun throwing snowballs, but it's scary getting chased."

Chris showed me his addition. I thought he had done a fine job of revising his ending, and I told him so. Chris agreed to lead a mini-lesson with the whole class the next day. First he read examples of different endings, as I had to him, and then he shared his first and second draft of *Snowballing*'s end.

Younger children can work on their closing lines, too; you needn't be a sixth-grade teacher to talk about endings. John is a third grader, and here is his draft, entitled "My Family":

My Family

My family likes to go swimming and fishing. My mom likes to swim. I like toys. We like ice cream.

My sister is six. I'm nine. My mom is 32 and my dad is 37. My dad's car is red. That is my family. And my dad likes to shot. I like it to

Just as with my sixth-grade class, I read several short pieces from *Ranger Rick*, putting each on the overhead as I read. I circled the last line or the last paragraph, depending on the piece. We talked about alternatives. Then I asked all the children to choose a draft from their writing folders that was complete and to look at the way they closed their piece.

John picked the draft above and did something very interesting. He circled the lines "And my dad likes to shot [shoot]. I like it to [too]" and moved them (via an arrow) to the space after "We like ice cream." He came up and showed me his revision. I asked, "Why did you choose to do this particular manipulation?" John said two things: 1) "My line 'That is my family' is a good ending line" (I thought to myself, *yes, it's a summary*), and 2) "These things [pointing to the lines he circled] are about what we like and that's up here [pointing to his first paragraph]."

As with Chris, I asked John if he would conduct a mini-lesson on endings. I wanted him to share his revision and tell the class why he decided to do what he did. He smiled and said, "Me?"

"Why not?" I asked.

"Well, all right," he said with a grin.

John and I made an overhead of his draft. The next day he introduced our writing period by asking the children to look up at the screen. "You'll see my revision," he began as he pointed to the lines he had circled. "I moved these lines for a couple of reasons. Who can guess why?"

Focused Lessons on Literary Forms: An Introduction
Frances Temple

As we all know, there are different sorts of writing that are appropriate to different purposes: lists for shopping, letters to thank or scold or sell or offer friendship, diaries to help us remember and to help us understand, advertisements, riddles, poetry. Some people call these different sorts of writing *forms*. While in primary school we are mainly concerned with promoting the children's confidence and fluency in writing, as the years go by, we expect students to develop the skill to handle a variety of forms.

Most of the forms we teach derive logically from the subject matter being studied. Children learn to write letters when they are writing to thank a parent volunteer for showing them how to make chapatis, or to ask a county supervisor to vote against garbage incineration. Children learn the form of sea chanteys when they are studying Columbus or Sir Walter Raleigh; they learn haiku as part of nature studies. This approach is usually more fruitful in getting children to write in a variety of forms than specific exercises, out of context, designed to make children write in a particular way. The child's purposes come first, but the teacher deliberately creates a setting in which writing in different forms can be perceived as useful. When this is done day in and day out, the students and teachers get a wide variety of writing practice.

Many forms are also picked up by children from things they read, from things that are read to them, and from each other. Often, the teacher can move this process along, and one way she can do this is through focused lessons.

Poetry
Frances Temple

Take poetry. It does not occur to some children to try to write poetry, much less that they might already be writing it. But in several ways, young children are natural poets. The three-year-old who calls the first motorcycle he hears a "chain saw bicycle" and the six-year-old who describes a stucco house as "made of stone dough" give us a glimpse of the earnest and intense mental effort that children make to find words for their perceptions. The baby gurgling to herself, "Ma ma ma mo mo mo moooooo-oooooo," and the eight-year-old sing-songing jump-rope rhymes over and over remind us of children's fascination with sounds and rhythms. And the first grader who slowly penciled the four words in Figure 2–2 could give us a lesson in choosing words economically and carefully.

What focused lessons can we devise that will encourage these three characteristics: 1) interest in phrases that evoke the right mental image, 2) interest in the sounds and rhythms of language, and 3) a careful economy in using language?

Focused lessons I find especially helpful teach poetic forms that require careful word choice (the examples I give are on cinquain and diamante forms). They include games and riddles that develop a sense of metaphor (for example, Smoke, described in the next chapter), and they take a child's piece of writing that has characteristics of poetry and enhance these characteristics through a poem-like presentation.

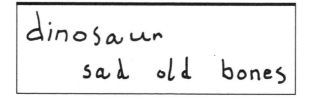

FIGURE 2–2 Four Words from a First Grader

CINQUAIN

This is how the cinquain form for poetry was introduced to a classroom of third graders.

The children came into class from gym, sweaty, tired, exhilarated, and complaining:

"Why do we have to come back here?"

"Why can't we just stay in gym all day?"

Teacher: What is it about gym that you like so much? What do you do there?

Students: We play basketball.

     Run around.

     Burn around corners.

     Smash into people.

     Yeah.

     Shoot baskets.

Teacher: Erin and Paul, could you write some of these things on the board, please? This is turning into a writing lesson. [*As the two children write, she continues.*] How does your body feel when you are doing all that running and jumping and . . .

Students: Hot.

     Sweaty.

     Breathing hard.

     I can hear my heart.

     Thirsty.

Teacher: I want us to try to make this into a cinquain. A cinquain has this form [*writing the form on the board*]:

Noun

adjective, adjective

three-word sentence

four participles

Noun

Who can give us a noun to start off with? What is this cinquain going to be about?

Students: Gym.

     Basketball.

     Gym.

Teacher [*writes "gym"*]: For now. Let's have two good adjectives to describe the noun.

Students: Sweaty.

     Thirsty.

Teacher: Good adjectives, but they are supposed to describe the noun. Is the gym thirsty?

Student: No. We are, when we are in gym.

Teacher: What do you all think? Shall we change the noun and keep the adjectives? Or keep "gym" and change "sweaty" and "thirsty"?

Students: Keep "sweaty" and "thirsty."

That's us.

Teacher [erases "gym" and writes "us"]: Okay?

[Students agree.]

Teacher: Now we need a three-word sentence about us (you) in gym.

Students: We like gym.

Everybody likes gym.

[Teacher writes it.]

Teacher: Now we need four participles—those are action words with -ing, like "singing."

Students: Jumping.

Running.

Crashing.

Smashing into people.

Dribbling.

Shooting.

Passing.

Teacher: We have lots of good ones to choose from. [*Writes the first four.*] Now we need one good noun to tie it all together. Do we have one we didn't use in the beginning?

Student: Basketball.

The teacher completes the cinquain on the board; it reads:

Us
Sweaty, thirsty
Everybody likes gym
jumping, crashing, running, smashing
Basketball

The teacher calls on a few children to read the cinquain out loud, and then says: "That's pretty good for a cinquain written by a committee. Can you each try one of your own? And make it even better?" Later the class shared some variations.

Kids
Sweaty, thirsty
Crazy about gym
jumping, running, crashing, smashing
Noise.

Ball
round, smooth
I grab it
bouncing, dribbling, passing, shooting
Basket!

For a child to learn the cinquain form and then use it only once or twice is marginally useful. Cinquain becomes a gimmick for learning the parts of speech, and it may produce a passable poem for the school newspaper. But used frequently, cinquain is one of those tools that can help children notice things more specifically, and find words to express what they notice. Because cinquain is so concise, it challenges the writer to choose words carefully, to arrange them in the order that will have the most impact (within a restricted number of alternatives), to think hard about the images conveyed by each group of words.

One way to call attention to one or more of these facets is to put a cinquain with some weakness on the board or overhead projector (the teacher can write it himself and present it as "A first draft I need help with," or can ask a child to volunteer a draft). The class can then work together or in pairs to rearrange word order, or to make the verbs more specific, the adjectives more image-provoking, and so on. The three-word sentence gives a lot of children trouble: at first most just write "I like. . . ." When children do branch out, saying things like "I grab it" (in the last cinquain) it's an occasion worth calling everyone's attention to.

DIAMANTE

Writing a cinquain gives a child a lot to think about; diamante adds one more dimension, and that is change. We suggest not introducing diamante until children are very familiar with cinquain and think of it as "user friendly."

Diamante has the following form:

Noun
adjective, adjective
three-word sentence
participle, participle/participle, participle
three-word sentence
adjective, adjective
Noun

The slash between participles is critical—it indicates a turning point, a line of symmetry or contrast.

Diamante provides a concrete way to summarize a story, to pose and answer the question: In a given story, how does the main character change from beginning to end?

The following diamante was the result of a long and interesting group discussion of *Jack and the Beanstalk*:

Boy
hungry, poor
Sell the cow!
yelled at, chased out/climbing, sneaking
Grab the hen!
quick, rich
Jack

The form lends itself well to describing metamorphoses: the appearance and sounds of a tree outside the classroom window, from winter to summer; the transformation of a tadpole into a frog; or the emergence of a praying mantis from a cocoon.

This poem reflects the children's understanding of Jack's transformation through taking initiative; everything before the slash is imposed on Jack; everything after is his idea or a result of his action.

Smoke: Tapping into Metaphor

Frances Temple

Smoke is a game we first saw in John Gardner's *On Becoming a Novelist* (Gardner, 1983). Besides being an entertaining way to fill miscellaneous stretches of downtime in the day, it develops a sense of metaphor. Once again, I will simply record one way it was presented to children and the results.

Teacher: I want each of you to think of a person—someone that you think the rest of us will have heard of—but don't tell anyone who you are thinking of. Write the name of your person on the top of your page and fold it over. I'll do the same.

[*When everyone is ready:*] I am going to ask you some questions, and I want you to answer them as if you were the person whose name you have written down. Here's my first question: If you were an animal, what kind of animal would you be? Just write down the first animal that comes to mind for your person.

Now, if you were a car, what kind of car would you be?

If you were a kind of music, what kind of music would you be?

If you were a bird . . .

weather . . .

a tree . . .

a musical instrument . . .

a fire . . .

After sharing their lists, each writer chose those metaphors he felt were truest for his subject, and rapidly converted them into a free-verse poem. Here are three very different sets of answers and the resulting poems. For the subject Harriet Tubman, a twelve-year-old student generated this list:

panther
tin lizzy
gospel
black crow
night-time, clear skies
stump

cricket
mouth bow
hidden fire

which became—

black crow singing gospel in the clear night sky, find me a
stump shaped like a panther. A cricket drones, or is it a
mouth bow?

Similarly, "Mike Munroe" yielded, first,

tiger
Taurus
hard rock
falcon
hot, sunny, humid
pine tree
hornet
Reeboks
guitar
bonfire

Then—

Tapping Reebok feet he plays good guitar; hot and humid
listening to hard rock in privacy.

Andres, 12

A favorite teacher, Mrs. DiRisio, started as

platiypus
convertible corvette
old rock
bluebird
sunny
apple
dragon fly
reeboks
dulcimer
campfire

Then became—

I'm a bluebird on a sunny day
I'm an apple tree in a field of hay
I'm a platypus swaying to some old rock
But last of all I am a dragon fly with my shining wings.

Mary Jo, 12

Showcasing and Polishing
Frances Temple

What we call showcasing is simply calling attention to poetic features in a person's writing. This can be done by putting the work on the board or on a transparency (with the author's permission, of course), and letting the children read and react to it. Often this is lesson enough; the children who like the work will emulate aspects of it on their own. Sometimes a group can help a child polish a piece of writing. If a child chooses to present her writing as poetry, showcasing often becomes a question of increasing the impact of a piece by cutting out unnecessary words, or changing the way the words are arranged on the page. Children can do this polishing without the teacher's help after a few modeling sessions like the one we will describe. The piece in Figure 2–3 was written by Liz, a third grader, as she looked at an old photograph. She and her classmates were studying U.S. history, life in the 30s.

Liz liked what she had written, but was not entirely satisfied with it. She agreed to write it neatly on an overhead transparency, and a group of children took up the challenge of shaping it into a poem. After Liz read the text out loud, we had the following discussion:

Teacher: Liz thinks this could be written up as a descriptive poem. It is almost right now, but it could be made better—a little clearer, more sharply focused. One thing you can do to help is to tell her which words you think she should definitely keep.

Students: "Cotton patch."

     "Vicksburg, Mississippi, 1936."

     "Three black people."

     All those two lines about the family.

     I like "his jean leg is rolled up . . ."

[*Liz underlined these phrases.*]

Teacher: Now let's rewrite the underlined phrases, maybe polishing them up a little. Is there something here that would make a good title?

FIGURE 2–3 Liz's Piece, "Vicksburg"

> there is a cotton patch in this picture with Takes place in vicksburg, mississippi in the delta area in 1936
> There are three ~~black~~ black people in this picture aman a women +a child that is Being held by the woman all of them are wearing Shabby cloths the man is holding a batch of cotton his right Jean leg is rolled up to his knee They all are wearing shoes except the child. The woman is wearing a Bress that is a tight Bray she has a couple short braids of the child has some to it looks like the girl is wearing a potato sack.

Soon we have:

Vicksburg, Mississippi, 1936
Three black people in a delta cotton field
A man, a woman . . .

Student: You say she's holding her child, but how? By the hand?

Liz: She's holding her on her hip, like a baby. "A man, a woman, and a child she is holding on her hip."

Teacher: What if you leave out "and"?

Liz: "A man, a woman, a child she is holding"—no—"a child on her hip," okay?

Teacher [*reading*]: "Three black people in a delta cotton field. A man, a woman, a child on her hip." How does it sound?

Students: Good.

But you might think the child is lying on her hip.

I wouldn't.

Put "with."

Liz: "With a child on her hip"? Okay.

The next discussion was about the shoes.

Student: In all the other pictures, people in the country don't have shoes. And I thought a lot of black people were even poorer than the white people, so why do they have on shoes?

[*Everyone looks at the photograph again.*]

Student: They aren't really picking cotton.

Teacher: How can you tell?

Student: They don't have a bag to put it in. The lady's dress is too tight. I think the man is just showing the cotton to the guy who is taking the picture.

Liz: Then what are they doing out in the field?

Student: Maybe they're on their way to church. Maybe it's Sunday.

[*After the line "Both have on shoes," Liz inserts a question: "Are they going to church?"*]

The last major discussion is about the child's dress. Some children looking at the photograph decide that it isn't a potato sack, that perhaps it is a flour sack. We talk about what each is made of, and why, about patterned flour sacks, and the XXX on Gold Medal flour.

After a few minutes, Liz thanks the group and ends the focused lesson. The children return to their own writing. At the end of class, Liz presents her final draft on the overhead:

Vicksburg, Mississippi, 1936

Three black people stand in a delta cotton field,
A man, a woman with a child on her hip.
The man holds a batch of cotton.
One leg of his pants is rolled up to his knee.
Both have on shoes (are they going to church?)
The woman is wearing a tight gray dress.
She has a couple of short braids and
the child does too.
The child's dress has words
and three little x's.

It used to be a flour sack.

Writers notice in order to write, and write in order to notice. Whether or not Liz and her friends created a piece of writing that could be called poetry, they looked at the photograph with all the discernment they could muster. In their effort to find the right words to convey what they saw, they began to see things they had not noticed before. In trying to decide about presentation, they brought to light some of their own feelings generated by looking at the picture: the question on line five makes explicit the feeling of mystery we get in looking at old photographs; the setting apart of the last line shows that it has special significance to the composer, perhaps because it is the single line that could make a child put herself in the place of the child in the picture.

Stories: Learning by Listening for Shapes and Forms
Frances Temple

In our primary class, we have just finished reading through Caldecott's *The House That Jack Built*, which begins "This is the house that Jack built," and ends with "This is the dog that chased the cat that killed the rat that ate the malt that lay in the house that Jack built." One first grader remarks that it went together like nesting blocks, and another, that it is like the song, "The Rattlin' Bog," which we sometimes sing in school:

The Rattlin' Bog

Hey, ho, the rattlin' bog, the bog down in the valley-oh!

In that bog there was a tree, a fine tree, a rattlin' tree
Tree in the bog and the bog down in the valley-oh!
Hey, ho, the rattlin' bog . . .

On that tree there was a branch, a fine branch, a rattlin'
    branch
Branch on the tree and the tree in the bog and the bog
    down in the valley-oh!
Hey, ho, the rattlin' bog . . .

On that branch there was a leaf . . .

On that leaf there was a nest . . .

In that nest there was an egg . . .

In that egg there was a bird . . .

On that bird there was a feather . . .

      (from Alan Lomax, Folksongs of North America)

I asked the children to write a verse in the same form, and since we had just been to a maple syrup farm, several of the children took this as their subject. Here's first grader Jed's:

Hirs the boy
Ho chops the
Wood to lite
The fire to

Bol the ship
To puot on the pakak.

Later we read "The Mouse Bride," a Japanese tale where an old couple, searching for the perfect wife for their adopted son (a mouse), turn first to the sun, then to the cloud that hides the sun, then to the wind that blows the cloud, then to the mountain that stops the wind, then to the tiny mouse that gnaws away at the mountain.

Before workshop, I suggested that some of the children might like to try writing a story with the same interconnectedness. Elizabeth, a third grader, who was working on a quilt at the time, wrote:

There once was a girl named Jill who was quilting
a quilt. She pricked herself with a needle. She said,
"You are the strongest of all, for you pricked my
finger." "No," said the needle, "the thread is stronger
than I for it can go through my head." Jill was
completely convinced that the thread was strongest of
all. So she turned to the thread and said, "You are
the strongest." "No, not I," replied the thread, "The
cloth is stronger, for it tangles me." Jill turned to the
cloth and said, "You are the strongest." "No, not I,"
replied the cloth. "Scissors are, for they can cut me."
Jill turned to the scissors and said, "You are the
strongest." "No, not I, fingers are, for they control
me." Then Jill looked at her fingers and said, "You are
the strongest." "No, not us," said the fingers. "You
are the strongest, for you control us." Then Jill said, "I
am the strongest, for I control the fingers which master
the scissors which cut the cloth that tangles the thread
that goes through the needle that pricked my finger."
Then Jill looked into the mirror and smiled and went to
bed and took a nap. While she was dreaming she had
a bad dream. When she woke up she wondered: A
dream is strongest, for . . .

When Elizabeth was reading her story to the class, one of the younger children started up and said, "I know a game like that!" For several days, during lunch, we had an epidemic of playing Rock/Paper/Scissors.

Talk about stories can also be focused on theme without structure. There is a familiar folk tale that goes something like this:

One bright summer morning, a peasant woman is walking to market, balancing on her head a jug of honey, which she intends to sell. "Today is my lucky day," she says to herself. "A rich gentleman is going to buy all my honey and with the money I will buy two little pigs, which I will fatten up and trade for a horse who will turn out to be a champion racer and I will enter him in a race and win a churn full of gold, and with it I will have huge wedding parties for my children." And at the thought of this, she jumps for joy, the honey falls, and she is as poor as ever.

The children were depressed by this theme: "I don't like these stories."

Teacher: Why not?

Children: They make the woman look silly.

I like the woman.

Teacher: Tell us what makes you like her.

Children: She's thinking of things her money will get for her children.

She's happy.

It's just sad because it doesn't work out.

Teacher: What could she do to make her hopes work out?

Children: It's not her fault.

She could try again.

Teacher: Let's try to write our own stories, using the same theme.

These two stories reflect the children's mood, as well as a good grasp of the theme.

Folk Tale Retold

(Sarah, second grade)

Once there was a little girl named Amanda. She was walking down the street with a cake on the top of her head yelling, "A cake for sale!" If I sell this cake I will get lots of money for it. Then I will buy myself a farm with all of the animals I like. But when everyone saw her with a cake on her head they laughed and laughed. One little boy laughed so hard he tipped over backward, dropping the eggs he was holding and knocking Amanda off her feet so there was a mess of eggs and cake. Amanda feeling very sad. Not rich. Just the same.

Don't Count Your Chickens Before They Hatch

(Elizabeth, third grade)

There once was a beautiful girl who was carrying a jug of milk. She was great at dancing. She thought, if I sell this milk I'll buy a beautiful dress and dance. I'll make so much money—she imagined she was on stage. She clapped her hands to the music—and then she dropped the jug of milk. She cried with dismay, "Now my milk is gone and I cannot buy a beautiful dress and dance to the music." Her thoughts left her as quickly as they came.

Tune in next time when she does something about it.

While heavy-handed harping on themes can kill a story, some awareness of themes can help students organize their own experiences. At circle one Monday morning several children were talking about what they had done on the weekend, and the teacher made the mistake of asking one dejected-looking child what he had done.

"We were going to Darien Lake, but my Dad had to work."

"You must have been really disappointed."

"Yeah."

"What were you most looking forward to doing there?"

The child launched into a catalogue of ride names, enthusiastically joined by some of the other children.

"Boy, you could write a whole story about this: all those wonderful plans, and then. . . ."

"Boom. Nothing. Just like the lady with the honey-pot."

Reading, Rereading, and Story Sense
Frances Temple

"Read it again! Oh, please read it again!" Teachers have long been pleased and puzzled by this clamor. Why do young children want to hear the same story over and over? If we knew, would it help us teach writing?

The following, as much a lesson for the teacher as for the children, took place in a predominantly first-grade classroom, early in the year. By trying to answer these questions, the lesson found its focus as it went along.

One day, during rest time, the teacher read the children "Ivan Tsarevitch and the Gray Wolf," chosen at random out of a book of Russian folktales. As soon as she was through, the familiar plea rang out. She read it again, and even, after some begging, a third time. The next day, the children asked to hear Gray Wolf again. Instead, the teacher read the next story in the collection, "Finist, the Bright Falcon," three times, as they requested. A few days later, the class ran through "Sister Alyonushka and Brother Ivanushka" four times. The repetitions in all the stories, compounded by many readings, seemed to please and reassure the children. The teacher fell into the habit of pausing and letting them fill in some predictable or easily remembered passages. Although from the children's point of view she was clearly doing something right, she worried about wasting time reading the same stories over and over. What were the children getting out of these stories?

Thinking back to being six, the teacher remembered lying on her bed after seeing a movie, trying to replay the whole film, frame by frame, in her mind's eye, mulling it over scene by scene, wanting to remember it forever. Was this the feeling some of these children had about these folktales? Could it be a longing people get when they are six, and just on the edge of literacy, but not yet literate?

And if so, what bearing might this have on the children's writing? Most of the children were just beginning to write about subjects of their own choosing. Because they were also just barely learning to control a pencil, the pieces they wrote were very short. On the other hand, their make-believe play showed they could invent and sustain complicated stories. Their skills of mental composition were thriving, even though their physical writing skills were not such that they could produce enough written text to require composing on paper. Guessing that it might be to this developing sense of composition that the folktales appealed, in part, with their magical elements set in such dependable structures, the teacher set about to see if the children's interest in folktales could be used in a way to practice and develop their composition skills, even though they were unable to write down the results themselves.

The children jumped at the suggestion that they invent their own "Russian" folktale and dictate it. They were told that since it would be a folktale—and they were folk as much as anybody—they should feel free to borrow, remember, change, or invent. Over a period of five days, they dictated the following story, arguing a good deal and correcting each other. The teacher did not suggest changes, but often went back and read over what they had already dictated so they would feel how the story was moving, and sometimes asked questions aimed at getting them to use more specific words. As scribe, she occasionally chose between paths different children wanted to take, at first letting the majority rule, and then asking the children who had previously been overruled to make decisions. Most of the children wanted to recreate a story close to those they had heard; they wanted their story to sound like an old Russian folktale. One young iconoclast wanted from the outset to write a spoof of a Russian folktale, but he was voted down a few times until the challenge of remembering structures began to entice him, and his suggestions began to fall within the tone the other children were trying to set. Here is the story the children dictated.

Day 1

Once long ago in a beautiful kingdom lived a tsar. He had three sons, named Peter Tsarevich, Alex Tsarevitch, and Ivan Tsarevitch. The older sons were ugly and lazy, but Ivan was handsome and did all the work. One day Peter Tsarevitch was walking on a path in the forest and he found a doe. He put a rope around the doe's neck and pulled her back to his father's house.

"I've caught a deer," he said to his father. "Shall I let it go or shall I kill it?"

"Keep it," said the tsar, who was very fond of deer.

The doe was set loose in the palace garden. There was a

high wall around the garden. The doe jumped and jumped, but to no avail. She couldn't get out of the garden.

Day 2

One evening, after a long day's work, Ivan Tsarevitch was sleeping in the garden. He was awakened by a soft voice. He looked around and saw that the doe was talking to him. "Ivan Tsarevitch," said the deer, "go to the thrice-ninth land beyond the thrice-tenth kingdom and fetch me the water of life, the water of death, and the water of happiness."

Ivan Tsarevitch looked at the deer and the deer looked at him with sad brown eyes. "I will do it," said Ivan Tsarevitch.

Ivan took three loaves of bread, three turkeys, and three pizzas and left the palace.

After many days of traveling he came to the edge of a swamp . . .

On these first two days the children dictated steadily for fifteen minutes. Their story was not copied exactly from any of the tales the class had read, although it included elements from several of them. Turns of phrase were remembered precisely, as were words they did not ordinarily use in conversation. By the third day, the children were no longer thinking carefully about what they were dictating; they were anxious to finish the story. There were puppets in the room, and the teacher asked them to go into groups and work the story up from where they had left off. The next section was dictated after two boys acted this scene out particularly dramatically, using puppets. All the children recognized that this was good stuff, and the story was rolling again.

Day 3

. . . As he stepped forward he sank, first to his knees, and then to his waist. He struggled but to no avail. Every move made him sink faster. Just when the quicksand reached his neck, a big hairy beast jumped out of the forest and across the quicksand, grabbed his collar, and dragged him out of the swamp.

"Thank you! You saved my life. I am grateful to you." panted Ivan Tsarevitch. "Who are you?"

"Just call me Gray Wolf," said the beast. "Where are you going?"

"I am going to the thrice-ninth land beyond the thrice-tenth kingdom to fetch the water of life, the water of death, and the water of happiness."

"Perhaps I can help you," said Gray Wolf.

And so he did. Gray Wolf took Ivan on his back . . .

Day 4

. . . The first stop was a hut with chicken legs which spun around and around in a circle.

"Turn your back to the forest and your door towards me," commanded Ivan.

The hut turned around and sat down. Ivan went in. Inside was Baba Yaga. Her eyes were on her chin; her nose was on her tongue.

"Foo, foo, foo! I smell the blood of a Russian. What did you come here for, young fellow?"

"I am going to the thrice-ninth land beyond the thrice-tenth kingdom to fetch the water of life, the water of death, and the water of happiness."

"Foo, foo, foo! Stand up, hut!"

The hut stood up dizzily. The door swung open. Ivan jumped out. He ran to a tree. Out of it flowed three streams of water . . .

Several of the children were emphatic that there should be three encounters with Baba Yaga instead of only one; the majority were ready to finish. All of the children participated in the dictation up through the Baba Yaga scene, but they were all agreeable when two children asked if they could draft the ending on their own. One of these two was a second grader and was willing to be scribe (see Figure 2–4).

FIGURE 2–4 The Draft of the Story

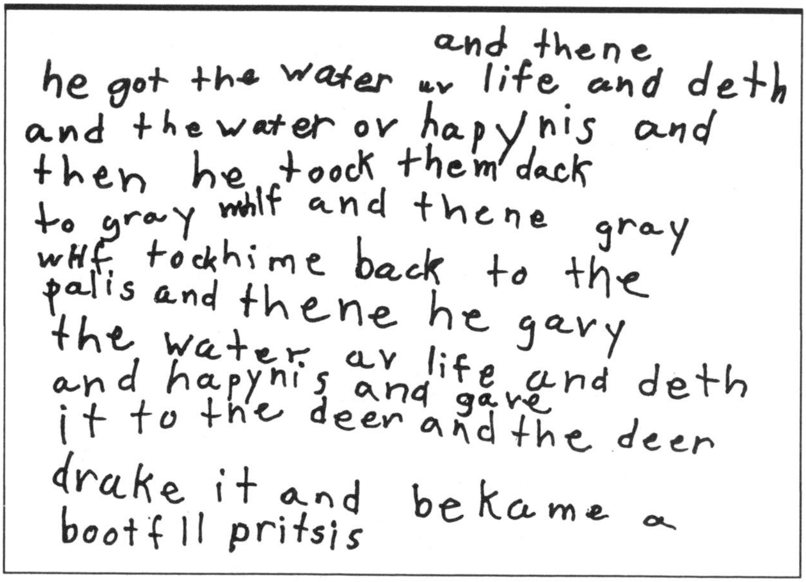

he got the water uv life and deth and thene
and the water ov hapynis and
then he toock them dack
to gray wolf and thene gray
wolf tockhime back to the
palis and thene he gavy
the water av life and deth
and hapynis and gave
it to the deer and the deer
drake it and bekame a
bootfll pritsis

Later, when the teacher read this over to the whole class, some of the children had questions:

Children: How did he know where the water was?

Baba Yaga told him.

Teacher: How did she tell him? What did she say?

Children: She said, "Follow your nose."

She said, "Follow your silly nose until you see an oak tree with water pouring out."

Teacher: That sounds like Baba Yaga talking, don't you think? Can we put it down?

Children: Put it in.

Teacher [*reading*]: ". . . and then he got the water . . ."

Children: What did he get the water in? You can't just carry water.

His hat.

He didn't have a hat.

Baba Yaga threw him a bucket.

And he held it up to the tree and the water ran in.

And they had to carry it very carefully not to splash it all out on the way home.

Teacher: Let me write that. [*Writing*] This is getting even better, don't you think, Jed and Juan? You wrote it well, and now it is getting even better.

Jed: Did I say that when they got to the palace the deer was almost dead?

Teacher: You didn't put that in the first draft, but we could add it in now. We should, shouldn't we? It does make the story more exciting.

Child: It does make you glad they got back.

Teacher: So Ivan Tsarevitch gets back to the palace and the doe is almost dead. What does he do?

Children: He cries.

Tears are running down his face.

He puts the deer's nose in the bucket.

Teacher: And then?

Child: That did it. She turned into a beautiful princess.

Teacher: Which is just what Jed and Juan wrote.

Children: "And they lived happily ever after."

No.

"For more years than storyteller can tell or pen can write."

The retelling of Gray Wolf suggested several things to the teacher. The first has to do with following the children's lead on what is interesting to them. If they want to hear a story five times, it may be more constructive to let them hear it and to find ways to follow up on their interest than to give in to teacher-image concerns by turning to something that might look more constructive to a visiting parent.

The second is that the group composing process offers learning opportunities that extend those afforded by individual composing and conferencing. Children who are not yet writing get to practice composition. Children hear aloud many of the possible choices of phrase that normally simply pass through the individual writer's mind. And the group composing process provides nonthreatening opportunities to model conference questions. It was after this lesson that the teacher began to hear children in workshop asking each other such questions as:

"How do you mean, 'he went'? Walking or riding?"

"What kind of voice did he say it in? Did he yell?"

Thirdly, the teacher was quite simply amazed at the children's ability to remember the structure of the folktales they had heard and to cluster different events around the same basic structure, making a new story. This ability seemed to be intuitively derived from hearing many similarly shaped tales and would seem to lay a good foundation for remembering stories, for inventing stories, and for seeing the story in situations encountered in daily life or in the imagination. The teacher felt she had stumbled on something that six-year-olds were especially good at and especially keen on practicing, call it composition or storytelling.

Story Writing and Dialogue
Kathleen Juntunen

It is rarely difficult to motivate children for story writing. They often have an idea for a beginning and are anxious to get going. Frequently, however, they get stuck somewhere in their writing and don't know what should come next, or perhaps are at a loss as to how to end the story. To help them keep moving in their writing, I introduce the elements of a story: setting, characters, goals, problems, episodes. An economical way to introduce the features is by using a story grammar (see Figure 2–5). I begin by reading a simple, short story. I like the Fox stories by Edward Marshall. These humorously written stories, told through animals, are slightly exaggerated, everyday situations familiar to the children.

For example, in the story "Fox in Charge," from the book *Fox At School* (Marshall, 1983), Fox (always the main character) brags to his animal friends that he wants to be a teacher when he grows

---

I. Where will your story take place?

II. What characters will you have in your story?

III. What will your main character's goal be?

IV. What problems/incidents will get in the way of your main character's goal?

Episodes:

1. _____

2. _____

3. _____

4. _____

5. _____

Ending: How will your story end?

FIGURE 2–5 A Simple Story Grammar

up because, he says, "It's an easy job." That very day, the teacher, Miss Moon (a cow), leaves the classroom and puts Fox in charge. Of course, pandemonium reigns, no one pays any attention to Fox, and his former bragging is disproved. Finally, the principal hears the racket and intervenes. He hauls the main perpetrator to the office and the class quiets down. Fox does get some redemption when Miss Moon returns and compliments him on how well behaved the students are.

After I read the story, each student is given a copy of the story grammar and we fill it out together. We note the fact that one story may contain several settings, and the setting change often signals a new episode. We also discuss the possibility of more than one goal and problem in a story. Then we all read another story together. The children work with a partner to fill out a story grammar and we discuss their ideas together. The more practice they have in analyzing stories, the better they become with their own writing.

When students are ready to begin writing their own stories, each is given a blank story grammar. I get them started by saying, "I know most of you already have ideas for your stories, and I would like you to fill out as much of the story grammar as you can. You may not know all the episodes or all the characters, but try to write the opening setting, the main character, and the goal or goals. If you think of any problems there might be reaching the goal, write those down too. Don't worry about parts you don't know right now. Many authors find ideas come to them as they write. You might be surprised where your story leads you as you are writing. Remember, this story grammar form is just to guide you in thinking out your story. Sometimes you will use only parts of it, and sometimes you won't need it at all. And if your ideas become different from what you wrote on the form, don't hesitate to change them."

At best, a story grammar can provide a sort of blueprint for a story and can enable a student to work on particular aspects like dialogue, lead, description, ending, without losing sight of the whole. In this sense, it is particularly useful to students who have started writing longer stories, or stories with several episodes.

In another lesson, the students and I discuss dialogue in stories. They usually conclude they like dialogue because it "makes you feel like you're in the story" and "makes the story move faster."

I begin by saying, "Today we'll try one way of getting conversation, also called dialogue, into your story. We'll use the story grammar outlines you have written. Often, if you act out your story with another person, you will discover some dialogue you may want to include. I would like to model this with one of you. Who would be willing to act out their story episodes with me for the class?" In Miss Trocke's third-grade class, Andrea volunteered.

Andrea and I are seated next to each other so we can both see her story grammar sheet. "Where does your story begin?"

"At home."

"And who are the characters in your story?"

"Me, my mom, Ann, Jess, Amy, and my guinea pigs."

"Okay. What have you written for the goal?"

"Selling all the baby guinea pigs."

"What are the problems in doing this?"

"They run away."

"I see that you already have written several episodes. The first episode says, 'White fur face & Black.' Tell us about it."

"Well, my guinea pigs are called White Fur Face and Black Fur Face and they have so many babies that my mom tells me I have to sell them."

"So now you have to figure out how to do that."

"Yes."

"Okay, let's pretend I'm your mother and we'll demonstrate for the class a conversation we might possibly have in this situation. I might say to you, 'Andrea, we *cannot* have all these guinea pigs around here. You are going to *have* to sell them.' Now what might you say to me?"

Andrea pauses for about a minute. I ask, "Well, how do you feel about what your mother says? What are you going to do?"

"Well, I could say, 'I don't know *how* to sell them.' "

"Okay, and your mother might answer, 'Well, I hope you figure out something!' "

Andrea pauses and I ask, "In your story, what have you decided to do?"

"I'm going to make a sign."

"And what does the sign say?"

" 'Guinea pigs for sale' . . . and the price."

"Where will you put the sign?"

"On my front lawn."

"Okay. Now you're on your front lawn with this sign, trying to get people to buy these guinea pigs. Go ahead and act that out."

Now Andrea gets into the swing of it and shouts, "Fresh guinea pigs for sale, $1.50 each!"

We continue through her episodes, and as the class watches, I notice some students scratching notes onto their papers.

When we are finished, Andrea feels she has some ideas for dialogue to include in her story.

"Boys and girls, you will all have a chance to act out your story. When you do, I'd like you to be thinking about the dialogue you use. See if you can get some ideas for your writing."

It takes only one modeling for the rest of the class to want to get into the act. The role playing does not always have to be done for the entire class. Small groups also work very effectively in having students help each other with their story writing.

Children love this role playing and always beg for more. It helps them clarify their thinking and gives them new ideas. In addition, it is a valuable demonstration of how they can include dialogue in their stories. Sometimes the children will write their story in play form as a result of the role-playing activity.

Author's Night

Kathleen Juntunen

It seems fitting to end this section on focused lessons with a lesson a friend taught me. Miss Austin, a first-grade teacher in my district, thinks school year's end signals celebration. The following activity was so successful, it has now become a tradition for Miss Austin's classes.

Authors' Night in Miss Austin's first grade was the culmination of the year's writing. It was held in their classroom in the evening so every parent could attend.

The children had written many pieces: stories, pattern books, social studies and science reports, biographies, autobiographies, letters, and poetry. Miss Austin helped each child select the piece to be read at the program. The children practiced by themselves and the class had one rehearsal. In addition, several students had small parts in conducting the program.

To begin, a student welcomed the parents. He then thanked the mothers who had done typing for the class, and me, the writing consultant. We were presented with certificates of thanks and small floral bouquets. A second student thanked the media teacher for taping the Authors' Night event and presented her with a bouquet. Next, a student briefly introduced the main part of the program, the readings by the authors. When the readings were completed, a student introduced me. I had been asked to speak to the parents about how they could encourage their children to continue writing. During this twenty-minute talk, Miss Austin took the children to another room for a "wiggle" break and read them a story.

When the students returned, Miss Austin and I presented awards in an Academy Award mode. Each child received unique recognition for a particular skill, for example, Funniest Book, Best Pattern Book, Best Story Beginning, Best True Experience Story, Best Biography, Best Illustrations, etc. Each child came to the front, where they were congratulated and given a handshake by me. Then Miss Austin pinned a paper apple on each youngster and gave each one a real apple. The children had been instructed informally to think of something to say after receiving the award. Sample comments were: "I will try to make my books funnier"; "Thank you for this fabulous Apple Award"; "I will try to write in my spare time"; "I am honored to have this great Apple Award."

The closing portion of the program was also explained by a student. Each child had written an About the Author page, and Miss Austin had compiled these into a booklet called "Authors' Day Autographs." There was a copy for each family. The students told the parents they could pick up the autograph booklets and circulate among the authors for signatures while cookies were being served.

Following this exciting evening, a letter was sent home to the parents asking for comments on the program, and some of the children were interviewed about their feelings concerning Authors' Night. The success of the evening can be judged by the following comments from the children and their parents.

From students:

- "It was pretty fun to listen to all the other kids' stories . . . and listen to the moms clap. I felt good when my mom and everybody was listening."
- "My favorite part was when I gave my speech. I liked the cookies."

From parents:

- ". . . an incredibly enriching experience for both students and parents. I felt like I was sharing a part of each of the children's lives! I was most impressed with how the students were treated as young professionals. What positive encouragement!"
- "I was sincerely impressed by the enthusiasm of the children about their stories. It seemed they were all so proud of themselves and their work! Instilling a zest for learning and self-confidence, I believe, is what this is all about!"
- "Everyone seemed to *know* they could write, and had the credentials to prove it (a printed bookful of stories)."
- "They gain self-esteem by knowing their precious work is respected."
- "It's beneficial to have the children learn to speak in front of a group early in their education. It's a fear so many adults never conquer."
- "Authors' Night was a great idea. It made the kids proud of all their hard work and the parents just as proud of them. This should be done every year."

REFERENCES

Calkins, Lucy McCormick. 1986. *The art of teaching writing.* Portsmouth, NH: Heinemann.

Cramer, Ronald L. 1978. *Writing, reading, and language growth.* Columbus, OH: Charles E. Merrill.

Gardner, J. 1983. *On becoming a novelist.* New York: Harper and Row.

Lomax, Alan. 1975. *Folksongs of North America.* New York: Dolphin Books.

Marshall, Edward. 1983. "Fox in charge." In *Fox in school.* New York: Dial Press.

WRITING ACROSS THE CURRICULUM

Introduction
Charles Temple

Teachers of writing to older students have long sensed that you have to know poetry in order to write it, that you have to be saturated in good descriptive writing to develop descriptive powers of your own. And while it is true that primary-grade children can produce unselfconscious poetry and description that dazzles us for its freshness, as education continues beyond third and fourth grades, in our experience, children need to draw more and more on a kind of reservoir of writing models that have been stored up from reading and from reflecting on reading.

In the early phases of the process approach to teaching writing, the importance of literature was not always emphasized. But today, many teachers and researchers of young children's writing are recognizing this neglect and are taking steps to correct it (see, for example, the writings of Jane Hansen and Ruth Hubbard, both of the University of New Hampshire, from which came so much of the early push for process writing in elementary school). In particular, the *whole language* movement has sought to integrate the teaching of reading and writing so that the two reinforce each other.

Sometimes in the process-writing approach there is a tendency to treat writing as an end in itself. Many teachers have taken the suggestion that children should write about things that are important to them to mean that children should write only about topics that they choose. This is understandable, as so many of the writing samples that have appeared in the literature about children's writing deal with children's out-of-school experiences. But to limit the content of the writing program to personal, out-of-school experiences is to pass up the great contribution writing can make toward sharpening our powers of observation and deepening our powers of reflection, especially as they relate to the natural, the social, and the cultural world—in other words, as they relate to the content of the school curriculum.

This oversight, too, has begun to be corrected in the new emphasis on *writing across the curriculum*, which is beginning to be felt in elementary classrooms (Fulwiler, 1987; Parker & Goodkin, 1987). We welcome this development because it captures the intellectual energy, the student-centered initiative, and the spirit of responsive teaching of process-writing programs and injects them into the rest of the school curriculum.

In the lessons that follow in this section, you will find that many walls have been broken down: between the writing program and the study of literature, between the language arts and the subjects of social studies and science, between the roles of teacher and learner, even between work and play. You will see writing, reading, talking, singing, acting, observing, performing, reporting all developed in units that have proved intensely interesting to the children who participated in them.

In sum, you will see a "second generation" process-writing program, a program with its emphases corrected, so that writing informs and is informed by everything else that happens in the school day.

Writing and Nature Study
Frances Temple

Nature studies are a staple of the elementary school curriculum and for good reason. At a time when young children are being introduced to the abstractions of number and letter symbols, nature studies are an ongoing link to the outside, observable world. A toad is as fascinating to a preliterate child as to a literate one. At the same time, the study of nature provides reasons to describe verbally, to read and to write.

Now wild geese return.
What draws them, crying, crying
all the long dark night?

(Roka)

Congratulations, Issa, you have survived to feed this year's mosquitos!

(Issa)

Don't waste precious time now, tagging
        along with me, Brother Butterfly.

(Issa)

Each morning, beginning in September, we have been reciting haiku verses such as these, adding a new one every few days. By Christmas the children know some twenty of them by heart, and we go on to other forms of poetry. There has been no need to discuss or analyze the haiku. Occasionally, throughout the year the children ask if we can do the haiku, and we recite them all. Although some roll their eyes—"Not again!"—they all seem proud that they can remember so much. The beauty and simplicity of form and thought inherent in these haiku affect the children as if by osmosis. Figure 3–1 shows a first grader's first writing attempt in workshop.

For fall Show and Tell, we ask children to bring in things they have found. (Later in the year it will be things they have made, and later yet, things they have read.)

Hello. There.
SLOW. Small. snaiL.

**FIGURE 3–1 A First Grader's First Attempt at
Writing in Workshop**

Often, after showing what they brought and telling how they
found it, children want to write about it in workshop. The questions they've been asked in circle help them develop a sense of
audience for their writing. (See Figure 3–2, a and b.)

In the fall, the class takes long rambles out of doors. Each
child has a nature notebook. Sometimes we stop and draw and
make notes (see Figure 3–3). Sometimes we make this into a
scavenger hunt. The assignment might be:

Find as many different kinds of seed pods as you can. Draw them and
label them if you can find out their names. For the older children: Describe how the seeds travel.

(Teachers carry plastic sandwich bags, which the children can
tape into their notebooks and use for collecting.) A sample written
response to this assignment is shown in Figure 3–4.

Or again:

Find all the insects you can. Draw them. Write down what they look like
and what they are doing.

(See Figure 3–5.)

**FIGURE 3–2 Two Examples
of Show-And-Tell Writing**

Hello there
Spider on the top
of the Jar.

(a)

I FOWNd a
SON WtH
a HOL IN IT
I fowND it
at- tHe-OSHIN
It is a lecKY SuoWN
tHe wars WosHt
UP-IN-tHe-SUNN

(b)

This is a butterfly sucking the honeysuckle.

FIGURE 3–3 Nature Notes

FIGURE 3–4 Scavenger Hunt Notes

Or:

What can you find living in the bark of a tree?

(See Figure 3–6.)

Later, in process workshop, a child sometimes decides to do a report based on his notes. Figure 3–7 is one such report.

Of course, what children mainly want to do outdoors is to run, not sit and sketch. This might be a time to introduce maps and directions, points of the compass, wind directions, the rudiments of tracking.

Maps and/or directions require a little more planning on the teacher's part than the other activities we've suggested. The children need to work in small groups or some get frustrated, if not trampled.

Here's an example of incorporating directions:

Find three willows in a row. From the middle one go north ten giant steps. Turn to the east. Walk thirty paces. You will find an animal burrow. Draw it in your book. Look for tracks. What might live here?

Figure 3–8 is a sample response.

FIGURE 3–5 Response to Hunt for Insects

FIGURE 3–6 Notes on Tree Creatures

FIGURE 3–7 Sample Report

Aphids are tiny insects that live underneath some leaves on plants. They are so small I need a magnifying glass to see them. They are shaped like little drops. The interesting thing about aphids is that they ~~to~~ make a kind of juice called honeydew that ants like to drink. So ants take care of them and take them over to good leaves to eat, and drink the juice.

FIGURE 3–8 Speculation on Animal Burrow

I think someting big lives here. Because a lot of durt is scraped off. Maybe a bager or a fox. No tracs, just a tonail scratch.

FIGURE 3–9 Children's Own Maps and Puzzles

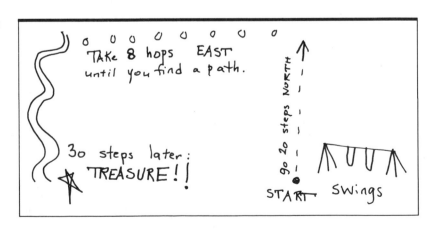

TAke 8 hops EAST until you find a path.

30 steps later: TREASURE!!

go 20 steps NORTH

START   SWings

FIGURE 3–10 Treasure Hunt

> 1. A brd cud lay a egg here.
> 2. go to the tire Swing and spin.
> 3. you have to kral thru.
> 4. Dig in the sand under a bucet.

Usually some children pick up on this idea and begin to make maps for each other, at recess or in workshop time (see Figure 3–9).

A variation is the treasure hunt format, where one written clue leads to another, and another. Figure 3–10 is a series two second graders wrote for some friends.

As winter closes in, we rely more heavily on films, *Ranger Rick Nature Magazine*, indoor pets, and the bird feeder.

If we are viewing the sort of nature film whose purpose is to convey information, I generally ask the children to take notes. In a rudimentary way, this practice gives the children a notion of the structure of expository prose, the sort of text designed to convey information. Later on, when they are reading articles in books or magazines for information, the ability to outline, to see the structure of the information presented, will serve them in good stead. At first, of course, a child may not be able to take in all the information he is being given. It is also impossible for someone who is just learning to write to take full notes. Still, whatever the children do write down they are usually proud of, both as writing and as new knowledge.

Figure 3–11 shows a first grader's notes on a film about penguins. Later, in workshop, this child wrote an illustrated book about penguins, using this information and some more that she

FIGURE 3–11 A First Grader's Notes on Penguins

> they walk or slide on ther tummuys. It's a fast way of geting around. and it would be fun. they eat fish. penguins crowd around the water and push one of them in the water to knonk if it's safe or not.

remembered. At my suggestion she asked some of her friends for their notes and used them too.

Figure 3–12 was written in workshop by a fourth grader after seeing a film on whales. In this piece of writing, Andrew gives information but presents it in story form—a sophisticated move.

Jared, a second grader, wrote the piece in Figure 3–13 after seeing *PIGS! PIGS!* is an art film rather than a strictly instructional film. Jared's piece is poetic, too.

Some children will want to see a film a second time to check or complete their notes. This is justifiable, and may be necessary to prevent frustration, although other children may be ready to go on to another activity. For those who would rather read, it is practical to have some reading materials around on the same topic as the film.

Winter is also a good time to bring in dead insects, to look at them under the microscope and draw them to scale. Most children can draw to a simple scale in first grade—I usually expand a picture of an insect or other creature onto a nine-square grid and have the children copy it, labeling parts. (See Figure 3–14.) This introduces children to the notion of scientific drawing and the careful observation it entails. It also introduces them to the idea of proportion and of coordinates, which will be useful for map-reading and other purposes later on.

> ## A Whale Birth
>
> A whale has just been born from it's mother. It was hard for the baby to break the cord that connects it to its mother but eventually it broke loose. The baby is having trouble swimming up to the surface for air. It is drowning down and down but the mother has come to help the baby whale. She sweeps under her baby and the baby is on her back. The mother swims up to the surface carefully but fast and the baby is safe.

FIGURE 3–12 Andrew's Reaction to a Film on Whales

Snorty is posing fo his portrait. He is a showing off smart aleck.

FIGURE 3–13 Jared's Response to *Pigs*

Observing and drawing may seem beside the point in a writing curriculum, but it is part and parcel of whole language development. Children do not write in a vacuum; learning to write is solidly intertwined with learning to notice, to remember, to question. The types of activities described above expose children primarily to a need for descriptive writing. Because this may be a new mode of writing for some of the children, it is good to provide them with some models. We read excerpts from great naturalists who are also fine writers: Jean-Henri Fabre, John Muir, and Tracker Brown, to name just three. I have come to expect that when my students have the leisure to choose their own topics during workshop time, some of their writing will reflect this inspiration. Some of the qualities these writers share and that I look for in students are a passionate interest in their subject, careful and accurate observation, and an ability to deduce understandings from what they observe. In the pieces of writing shown in Figure 3–15 (a through c), at an elementary level each writer has succeeded in at least one of these areas.

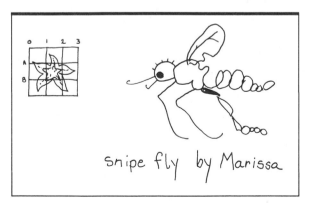

snipe fly by Marissa

FIGURE 3–14 Drawing with the Aid of a Nine-Square Grid

BeS
BaBeS r coLad Lrvus
Muthr Bes doaN Go
ot to Gut Fod
uth r Bes uot to Gut
Fod. the coeN Be is LaGr
is Brecus the LAags

Bees
Baby bees are called larvas.
Mother bees don't go
out to get food.
Other bees go out to get
food.
The queen bee is larger.
It's because she lays eggs.

(a)

gislings sum time get etin bie racoos.
or snaping tritls eat them or a flud
wushing the egg. They ol are fuse (fuzz.
and coot. and i just wot to pet them
and they cen fool and do not get hert
and they cen soim rite a wae.

(b)

Sam is a very sleek Guinea pig that is
Jumpy. He is male and has 4 sharp teeth.
I figure that sense he has four toes on
the front and three in back that
he must use his front more. His
eyelashes are about an inch. (long)
He eats corn and grain. He is
Black, Tan, White.

(c)

FIGURE 3–15 Observing, Writing, and Understanding. (a) "Bees." (b) By Johanna, Age 6. (c) By David, Age 8.

Writing and the Class Play: Literature in Action

Frances Temple

One day I took my class of first through third graders to a dress rehearsal of *A Midsummer Night's Dream* at our local college. After the play we tried to remember the most vivid parts, the moments that worked best. The children were familiar with this form of positive recall both from reflecting each others' writing in peer conferences and from their own plays, where the audience was always asked to "hold up a mirror" for the actors after a scene. As a way of helping the children extend their memory of particular characters and find more descriptive words, I taught them the cinquain poetry form, and we tried writing cinquains about some of the characters.

Titania
proud, beautiful
she loves children
dancing, mocking, angry, talking
Queen

Oberon
wicked, shiny
tricks the queen
hiding, laughing, making mischief
Master

Robin
mischievous, devilish
does Oberon's tricks
screaming, jumping, disappearing, bewitching
Puck

Bottom
clumsy, loud
he loves Titania
bragging, posing, bossing, braying
Ass.

The children were very excited by the play. I told them that the actors had to spend a lot of time in a room below the stage waiting to go onstage, and they came up with the idea of writing to the actors "so they'll have something to read while they wait." Figure 3–16 presents some of the letters that were delivered before that night's performance.

Midsummer kicked off an acting fever. The children wanted to do their own Shakespeare play. I found a shortened version of *The Tempest* in Albert Cullum's *Shake Hands with Shakespeare*. As we read it together, I highlighted the lines the children liked best. We talked about the explorers who had gone out to the New World at the time of Shakespeare and read some of the tales they brought back. We looked at old maps decorated with mysterious creatures. We wrote cinquains about various characters in *The Tempest*:

Ariel
gentle, magic
weaving Prospero's webs
floating, enchanting, scaring, disappearing
Sprite

FIGURE 3–16 Three Letters to Actors

Dear Oberon,
I loved your funky face and your wicked ways.

(a)

Dear Puck,
or do you preferr to be called Robin? you were great the way you screemed and jumped like a frog.

(b)

Dear Titania,
You were beautiful and very queeny with your chin up. Your dress floated.

(c)

Miranda
spunky, curious
amazed by Ferdinand
following, defending, working, loving
girl

I edited the script further, being sure to leave in the high-lighted sections. We assigned parts and got to work on lines. As the children worked on lines, we talked about meaning constantly.

"Why is she saying this?"

"Why is he so angry?"

"What could 'flamed amazement' possibly mean?"

If a passage seemed too long to a child, she would ask me if she could cut it. I would ask if something essential was being said. We would decide on the minimum of words that needed to be kept to preserve the meaning of the passage. We would check our decision with other students. The following are some conversations among actors overhead during practice:

Child 1: Okay. Listen. See if this makes sense: "I escaped on a keg of wine that the sailors threw overboard." I put "threw" instead of "heaved," okay? Or can I just say "I escaped on a keg of wine." How would that be?

Child 2: How did you escape?

Child 1: I floated to shore on a keg of wine.

Child 2: Why don't you say that?

Child 1: "I floated to shore on a keg of wine."

Child 2: Okay. That's good. That sounds good. Show with your arms how you were hanging on. Yeah!

Child playing Ferdinand: "If you are not already married and your affection not gone forth, I'll make you queen of Naples." I can't say that!

Other student: Ferdinand talks that way because he's a nerd. So you shouldn't change it. It won't be funny if you change it.

As the play began to shape up and the children began practicing on stage, those not in the scene being practiced would sit at the back of the auditorium with pencils and pads and write notes to the actors. These notes were modeled on the comments we use in a writing conference: the children were instructed to reflect what they saw—to note down gestures that worked well, lines well spoken—and to suggest possible improvements (see Figure 3–17, a and b).

FIGURE 3–17 Notes to
Actors

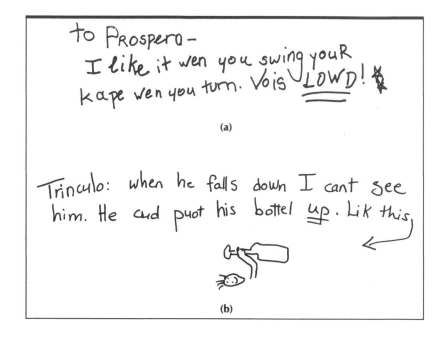

to Prospero –
I like it wen you swing your
kape wen you turn. Vois <u>LOWD</u>!

(a)

Trinculo: when he falls down I cant see
him. He cud puot his bottel <u>up</u>. Lik this,

(b)

By taking notes on individual scenes we were able to let the actors try a whole scene before breaking for comments. Keeping quiet and writing notes rather than blurting out comments was difficult for the children; it required a lot of self-discipline. But the practical value of taking notes was clear to everybody: the notes helped the children remember comments they wanted to make until the end of each scene. The performing children appreciated both the comments and the fact that they weren't interrupted during a scene.

"We need invitations!"

What information did we need to put on the cards? The basics, time and place, were old hat to the children because of birthday invitations. The idea of curtain time was new. One of the children wanted to add "grown-ups only," because at our earlier plays there were so many younger siblings running around that the actors had had a hard time making themselves heard. The class discussed this problem and decided against banning children.

"We could put up a sign saying 'Keep your children quiet!' " one suggested.

"It doesn't sound friendly."

"We could explain the reason."

Several children promised to work on it. They came up with a sign (Figure 3–18) and a standard playbill (Figure 3–19).

Please keep the little children quiet if you can so you can hear the play. It is a VERY GOOD PLAY! Love, the Actors

FIGURE 3–18 Sign

FIGURE 3–19 Standard Playbill

Because the first scene (the shipwreck scene) depended on darkness and flashes of light for its dramatic effect, the children were anxious that all the doors be kept shut. They eventually decided to add to the program a word of caution about being late (Figure 3–20).

"But if somebody comes in late they won't know what's going on." I told them that theater programs often include a synopsis of the story to help latecomers figure out what is going on, and several volunteers agreed to try their hand at writing one. This is the joint effort of three of the children:

The story of the Tempest goes like this. A man named Prospero and his daughter Miranda have been shipwrecked on an island for years. They wrecked when Miranda was a baby. Prospero is a magician. He likes to read. Caliban is a monster who lives on the island. He is mad with everybody, especially Prospero. Prospero yells at him and makes him chop wood. Ariel is an air spirit who serves Prospero and helps him play tricks on people. Prospero sees the King's ship passing and makes a storm so that the Prince will wash up on shore and fall in love with Miranda. Which he does. His name is Ferdinand and he is a nerd but Miranda loves him. Two sailors wash up on the island too, in a different place. Caliban finds them and thinks they are gods. Prospero sets Ariel free and decides not to be mean to Caliban anymore. He gives up magic.

The first scene is the shipwreck of Prince Ferdinand's ship. . . .

As we were making out invitations, a child suggested we invite the actors from *A Midsummer Night's Dream* "because they're

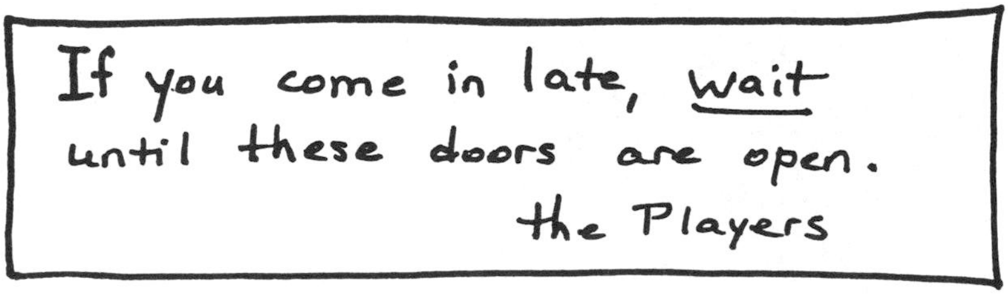

FIGURE 3–20 Sign for Latecomers

the ones that gave us the idea." During writing workshop time several letters were written to go with these invitations (see Figure 3–21). The children also wrote notes to parents and friends who had sent in props or costumes (Figure 3–22).

I called the local paper and a reporter came by to interview the children about the play. He asked sensitive questions, drawing

FIGURE 3–21 Letter to Accompany Invitation

Dear Puck,
  When we went to Midsumer we likt it a Lot. Will you come to the Tempest. If you have any green hár spray lefd bring it. Love,

FIGURE 3–22 Letter to Costume Giver

Dear Mr. Miller,
  Thankyou for sending the gold cape. It looks good on me. Better then the purple, you'll see.

FIGURE 3–23 Kindergartners' Sign

The Mysterious Play
You never know what it's going to be.

the children out to explain their characters. Unfortunately, he was called away on another assignment and never got the article written up, but his time with them was a good lesson in interviewing, which we were to remember and discuss later when the children themselves were ready to interview others.

Producing *The Tempest* required as much reading and writing on the students' part as they would have done in a more routine classroom, and it provided an interesting context for expanded language use. Our first audience was a kindergarten group, and I was happy to see the sign in Figure 3–23 stuck up in their room a few days later, evidence of a continuing ripple effect: Not only were the younger children putting on plays, they were writing about it.

Writing to Explore History

Frances Temple

Left foot, peg foot, carry on to freedom.
Follow the drinking gourd.

Mysterious words. By the time the children speculated about what these words meant to the people who made them up and to the people who sang them, we were launched into a study of the Underground Railroad.

Coming home from the library, loaded down with books, magazines, maps, and miscellany, questions came to mind. What writing skills can the children practice in the course of this study? What forms of literacy are useful to an understanding of history? What resources do we have?

There are songs, which they can learn as poems and expressions and riddles. Songs can be used as a reading text. The children can learn not only to sing but to write songs. There are stories, told and written, proving that the spoken or written word can make times past come alive again. The written stories can give the children examples of powerful narrative writing. The stories they hear told are sometimes ones they want to put down in writing themselves. There are, above all, poignant dramatic situations with which the children can empathize, leading them to dramatize, to invent dialogue, to flesh out in the imagination the bare facts that have come down to us.

USING SONGS

Follow the Drinking Gourd

When the sun comes up and the first quail calls,
Follow the drinking gourd. For the
old man is waiting to carry you to freedom.
Follow the drinking gourd.

Now the river bank'll make a might good road,
The dead trees will show you the way
Left foot, peg foot, travel on to freedom
Follow the drinking gourd.

Now the river ends between two hills.
Follow the drinking gourd.
And there's another river on the other side.
Follow the drinking gourd.

(Traditional)

Wade in the Water

Wade in the water
Wade in the water children
Wade in the water
God's gonna trouble the water.

If you get there before I do
Tell my friends I'm coming too. . . .

(Traditional)

By and By

By and by, Lord. When the morning comes
All the saints our God is gathering home
To tell the story how we've overcome
And we'll understand it better by and by

(Traditional)

The Rock Island Line

The Rock Island Line is a mighty good line
Oh, the Rock Island Line is the road to ride
The Rock Island Line is a mighty good line
If you want to ride it, got to ride it like you find it
Get your ticket at the station for the Rock Island Line.

(Traditional)

We printed the words of several songs into booklets with space at the top of the page for illustrations. We gave them to the children once they knew the words of the songs practically by heart, as reminders. The song words made a reading text that the beginning readers could decipher by matching remembered words to printed ones. Although the words were not as simple as those in a primer, the children already knew their meaning and quickly learned to recognize them in their booklets. The younger children read over their song words many times while deciding on appropriate illustrations.

The children began by making up additional verses to songs they especially liked. For example, to complete "If You Miss Me at the Back of the Bus":

If you miss me in the cotton-field
If you can't find me nowhere

Step right in to the Oval Office
I'll be working right there.

(Paul, 8)

Though I had not planned it this way, children began to get a sense of songs as not just an expression of what is going on at a particular time but also as a way to influence history.

Later, these same children wrote several anti-war songs that seem inspired by this perception:

What the world needs now
Is beans and rice and pizza
Beans and rice and pizza
That's what the world needs now
One thing we don't need
Is guns and bombs and missiles
There's too much killing
In the world, anyhow.

STORIES: HEARING, TELLING, ACTING, AND WRITING

There are many fine stories having to do with the Underground Railroad. Many of these are not written down in such a way as to be easily read to children, some because they are too gruesome or tragic, some because they are too wordy. Our librarian did find several good easy-reading books on the subject and brought them in so the children could do some research on their own, but I gleaned many stories from an old back issue of *National Geographic*, from history books, and even from fictional sources with a ring of truth, such as *Uncle Tom's Cabin*. I told or read the children these stories, and we built on them, in various ways. Let's illustrate with the story of Box Brown, who was shipped by his friends in a packing crate from Delaware to Ohio and lived to tell the tale. As we were finishing lunch, I told them this story, which I had read in the *National Geographic*. They had a lot of questions:

"How long was he in there?"

"What did he eat?"

"How did he go to the bathroom?"

"What if they picked up the box and just left him upside down?"

We tried to guess answers to these questions. Later, when we were playing Still Pictures, I asked the children to do a picture

of Box Brown. Still Pictures is a theater game that serves to remind students of a scene and helps them elaborate it in a simple
way. The title for a Picture is declared, in this case, "The Shipping
of Box Brown." Each child tries to think of something in the
picture she can be. As a child thinks of something she raises her
hand, and at a nod from the teacher calls out a word to identify
her part and takes her position in the picture, holding very still.
The children add onto the picture one at a time until everyone
who wants to is taking part. Figure 3–24 shows what we got with
"The Shipping of Box Brown":

"Box!" (1)
"Brown" (2)
"Nail in the box" (3)
"Straw" (4)
"Mail Checker" (5)
"Delivery man" (6)
"Baggage cart" (7)
"Bottle" (in hand of drunk)
"Drunk" (sitting against box)
"Train"
etc.

Children can't hold such a complicated still picture for more
than about three minutes. After they were back in their places, I

**FIGURE 3–24 The Shipping
of Box Brown**

decided to follow up on some of the ideas the children had shown and see if we had the makings of a dramatic scene.

"So, Tony, you were a drunk. Why were you leaning against that box?"

"I got tired. It was in the sun. Nice and warm."

"Then what happened?"

"Well, I heard a little rustling in the box. I thought it was mice. Then I heard a sneeze. It didn't sound much like a mouse."

"Were you going to tell anybody?"

"Yeah!"

"Why?"

"If it was a runaway in there and I told the station master, I might get some kind of reward."

"Yes?"

"So he gets up—"

"I get up and I call over to the station master—"

"And, station master, what do you do?"

"Well, I come over with a . . . to open the box."

"Crowbar."

"Now, let's say a friend of Box Brown is there at the station and he wants to stop the station master before he opens the box . . ."

"Me!"

"Me!"

"You try it, Steph."

"Well, if it ain't old man Silas! You still helping out the law, Silas? Silas and his bottle been tracking down runaways all over the coast. Haven't caught one yet, but he's seen aplenty. Sees 'em under ever bush. Sees 'em when they ain't there. Come on, Silas. Let me buy you a drink. You, too, station master. . . ."

Later I asked some of the children if they wanted me to read them the story just the way I had found it in the *National Geographic* (1984). They did, and they were able to follow it very well, even pointing out things we had changed. I think that the style might not have held their interest if we had read the story before telling and interpreting it.

A first grader who up until then had only written labels for pictures wrote what's shown in Figure 3–25 in workshop that week.

Many other stories sparked the children's imaginations and touched their hearts. Figure 3–26 was written by a first grader in workshop time after I had told a story from *Uncle Tom's Cabin*.

Developing stories the way we did with Box Brown gave the children practice in finding and expanding the drama in a situ-

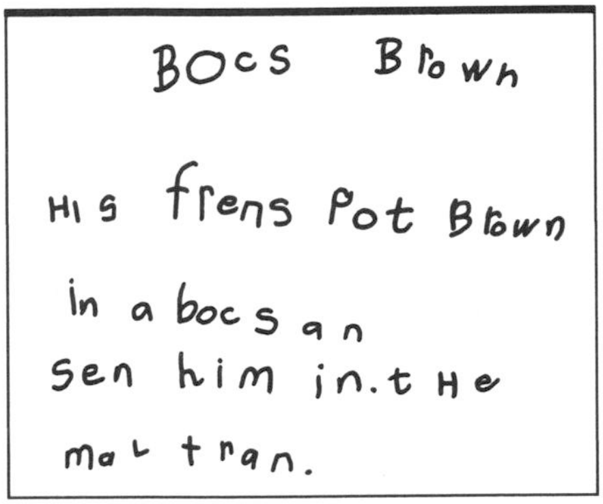

BOCS BRown

HIS frens Pot BRown

in a bocs an
sen him in.t He
mɑᴸ tRɑn.

**FIGURE 3–25 A First Grader's Writing
in Workshop**

ation. Still Pictures is a manageable way to begin this process,
by focusing the children's attention on a scene. The exercise can
be left there or it can be used as the basis for a shared make-
believe that can take life from the scene, as we have seen above.
A further step would be to help the children structure a dramatic
presentation on the basis of one of these scenes or stories.

This is a popular activity and one that develops language
learning on several fronts that are particularly important to children just learning to be writers.

The first is that both as actor and as writer the child needs
to develop a sense of audience. He learns to make a distinction
between ideas that are only in his head and ideas he has com-
municated to an audience. Response to a dramatic presentation
is usually more immediate and noticeable to a child than response
to a written piece.

A second front is that the children start listening more closely
to the ways people express themselves. Having to create dialogue
makes one very aware of the words and sounds people actually
use. This makes for vivid writing.

Thirdly, structuring a story for dramatic presentation is good
practice for structuring written stories. The acting/improvising
medium is in some ways more flexible than writing, especially for
the child with slow handwriting. Sequencing the action effectively
becomes very real to children as they devise a play. In dramatizing
stories, it becomes important to look for moments where decisions are being made, moments of suspense when the outcome
hangs in the balance, or moments when the wills of two protag-
onists are in conflict. A story or a play is most often built out from

FIGURE 3–26 "Eliza and Her Child" by Elisa, January 31, 1985

Eliza had a child. The child was going to be sold so she was running away with her child. She ran across the Ohio River when the ice was cracking. She had to run from piece to piece. The slave catcher could not get her and her child because the Ohio River was water now and they did not have a boat and they could not swim; it was too deep.

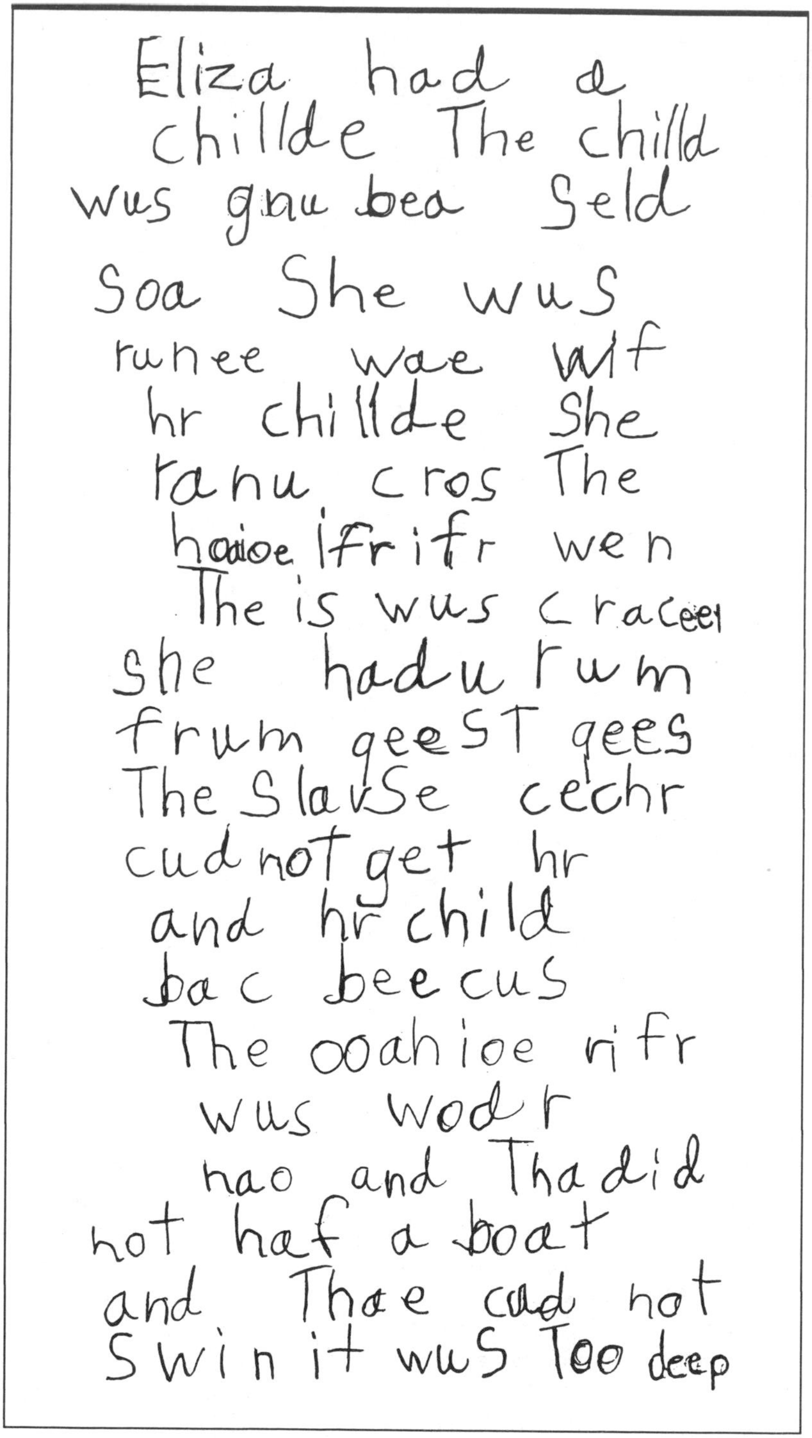

Eliza had a
chillde The chilld
wus gnu bea Seld
Soa She wuS
ruhee wae wif
hr chillde She
ranu cros The
haioe lfrifr wen
The is wus craceel
she hadu rum
frum qeeST qees
The SlavSe cechr
cud not get hr
and hr child
bac beecus
The ooahioe rifr
wus wodr
hao and Tha did
not haf a boat
and Thae cad not
Swin it wuS Too deep

one of these pivotal moments; children then devise earlier scenes to let the audience understand the situation, and add on later scenes to bring out the results of what happened in the pivotal scene.

In presenting for dramatization the story of Harriet Tubman, Judith Seto, author of *The Young Actors' Workbook*, chooses the moment when Harriet makes an excuse to her mother and goes and joins her brothers in the field. There she tells them she is leaving and tries to persuade them to come with her. This scene was developed at length by a group of children, aged seven to nine, who went off by themselves to work on it. I asked the brothers to think of three good reasons why they wouldn't go, and asked Harriet to try to talk them into changing their minds. The dialogue they worked up went something like this:

[*Rit and Harriet are hoeing around the bottom of a row of corn stalks. Harriet stumbles and sways, then catches herself.*]

Rit: What's the matter, girl?

Harriet: Another one of these sleepy fits. It's like I can't shake 'em off no matter how I try.

Rit: Go lie down in the shade. If I see anybody coming I'll get over there and get you on your feet.

[*In another part of the field Harriet comes upon her three brothers, Robert, William Henry, and Benjamin.*]

Robert: What you doing here? You not supposed to be here.

Harriet [*hoeing*]: Just working. Just like you.

[*They work a while in silence.*]

Harriet: I'm leaving. Tonight. I won't tell Rit. I want you all three to come with me.

Benjamin: Hat, we can't. We'll get lost. We don't know where to go.

William Henry: They say patrollers'll catch you before you can get anywhere.

Robert: They got dogs.

Benjamin: Dogs that can smell where you been even when you not there.

Robert: You saw that bite on Jacob. Hattie, you crazy.

Harriet: I'm going. I'm ready. I know how to find my way.

Benjamin: How will you find your way?

Harriet: By the stars and the moss. By the rivers and hills.

Robert: What about the dogs?

Harriet: Dogs can't smell through water can they? There are ways to fool dogs.

William Henry: Can you fool patrollers?

Harriet: I can try. I think I'm smarter than they are. But you can't plan everything ahead. Sometime you just got to go.

Benjamin: I'll go with you Hat.

Robert: Me too.

William Henry: We'll all go.

After working on this scene and presenting it to the rest of the class, the children asked if they could work on a scene that would take place after the four had escaped the plantation, as they travelled north. They went next door to work alone.

About twenty minutes later, I realized all hell was breaking loose in the adjoining room. When I was able to go and investigate, I found that the children were still heavily involved in the scene, but no longer as actors. Two had become alligators, two were truly terrified, and one seemed to be dead. This brought on a long discussion of the differences between acting and pretending.

Children: In pretending, you just do it.

You don't have to show anybody what you're thinking.

Teacher: And what about acting?

Children: Acting—you have an audience.

You have to show the audience what's going on.

Teacher: How can we make this pretending into acting?

Children: Not run around so much.

Really have an audience.

If you go out in the hall, the audience won't know what's happened.

Teacher: What do you really want to show the audience in this scene?

Children: That they get attacked by dogs.

And alligators.

And a slave catcher stops them and asks for their papers.

Teacher: It sounds like you have three parts to this scene.

Later, after they had worked on it a while, the children were able to find logical connections between parts of the scene. "Why don't Harriet and her brothers just jump off the road and hide in the bushes when they see the patroller coming?"

"They're scared the alligators will get after them again."

"Can one of you say that so the audience will know why you are hesitating?"

Keeping in mind the three objectives of audience awareness, dialogue building, and story flow, the teacher can encourage the children and help them see things in their work that move it in a good direction—changes that make the action clearer to the audience, dialogue that makes the characters more real, and transitions that are logical.

The following story, written by a third grader during process writing time, illustrates the way this unit of study generated a topic for writing and how sensitive a young child can become to audience, to dialogue, and to story flow.

First Station

It's hot in the desert; Tom works hard in slavery. The sun is out and shines on the sand. Tom is barefoot. One day he decides to escape.

He made sure no one was looking and started to run. He ran and ran and didn't stop until he came to a pile of leaves and a couple of sticks. He made a roof and lived four days under that roof.

He was eating a fish and he heard a horse neigh. Could it be true, someone was coming to get him? He ran behind a bush. The horse stopped. Tom peeked through the bushes. The man said: "I see you. Come on out of there. Hop in." It was a friendly voice. Well, it really made Tom feel good. So he climbed in and the man said: "Where to?"

"Anywhere in the North," said Tom.

REFERENCES

Beilenson, Peter, trans. 1958. *Four seasons of Japanese haiku.* Mt. Vernon, NY: Peter Pauper Press.

Blockson, Charles. 1984. Escape from slavery: The underground railroad. *National Geographic* 166: 3–39.

Brown, Tom. 1978. *The tracker.* Englewood Cliffs, NJ: Prentice Hall.

Cullum, Albert. 1968. *Shake hands with Shakespeare.* New York: Citation Press.

Fabre, Jean-Henri. 1921. *Fabre's book of insects.* New York: Tudor Publishing Co.

Fulwiler, Toby, ed. 1987. *The journal book.* Portsmouth, NH: Boynton/ Cook.

Hansen, Jane. 1985. Skills. In Jane Hansen, Thomas Newkirk, and Donald Graves (Eds.), *Breaking ground: Teachers relate reading and writing in the elementary school.* Portsmouth, NH: Heinemann.

Hubbard, Ruth. 1985. Drawing parallels: Real writing, real reading. In Jane Hansen, Thomas Newkirk, and Donald Graves (Eds.), *Breaking ground: Teachers relate reading and writing in the elementary school.* Portsmouth, NH: Heinemann.

Lomax, Alan. 1975. *Folksongs of North America.* New York: Dolphin Books.

Muir, John. 1901. *Our national parks.* Cambridge, MA: Houghton Mifflin.

Parker, John, and Vera Goodkin. 1987. *The consequences of writing.* Portsmouth, NH: Boynton/Cook.

Seto, Judith. 1979. *The young authors' workbook.* New York: Grove Press.

Stowe, Harriet Beecher, 1981. *Uncle Tom's Cabin.* New York: Bantam Classics.

CONCLUSION
Charles Temple

From setting up a process-writing classroom to celebrating young authors: we have reached the end of this book. The reader who has not tried teaching writing by a process-centered, student-centered method should have found in this book the essential practical information necessary to get started. The reader who wants more information about what to expect in children's writing—the nature of children's writing growth—is encouraged to consult Donald Graves (1983), Lucy Calkins (1986), Ann Haas Dyson (1985), or our own *The Beginnings of Writing* (Temple, Nathan, Burris, and Temple, 1988). Fortunately, in all parts of the United States there are regular summer workshops conducted under the auspices of the National Writing Project (for more information, contact Dr. James Gray, National Writing Project, School of Education, University of California, Berkeley, California 94720). In these workshops it is possible to work on your own writing, learn methods of teaching writing, and (usually) practice these methods with children under the direction of others experienced in the approach.

We also hope that teachers who are experienced in teaching children to write will have been inspired by this book to try new departures. The methods described here are very much in a state of evolution, and in trying them out you should feel free to modify them as your judgment dictates.

In any case, we have put into the first section the gist of what we offer in our own workshops on process writing for elementary teachers. These workshops have gotten hundreds of teachers off and running in the method.

The focused lessons we have included are only a beginning list; so are the lessons on writing across the curriculum. The lessons described in Section 2 work—each has been tried successfully with a variety of students. Nevertheless, the topics of these lessons will not be appropriate for every group of students; conversely, there are many more topics that would be appropriate for focused lessons than space has permitted us to share. We listed several such topics, but the active reader will have thought of others.

Section 3 contains only a sampling of lessons that have been taught, or might be taught, that put writing to use across the curriculum. They may have struck the reader as a little idiosyncratic. Indeed, Frances lives in a town where the Underground Railroad came through; she also plays guitar and sings, and teaches children's theater in the afternoons. Other teachers play sports, are skillful photographers, know how to make sausage, or can recognize scores of species of birds. Any and all of these interests (multiplied by those of the students) can inspire interdisciplinary writing lessons just as interesting as those here—in their own setting, perhaps more interesting. This last section, then, should be considered an invitation, as we hope our whole book will, to take stock of your own interests and your students' interests and develop the most promising possibilities *you* have to use writing in exploring and reflecting on life itself.

REFERENCES

Calkins, Lucy McCormick. 1986. *The art of teaching writing*. Portsmouth, NH: Heinemann.

Dyson, Ann Haas. 1985. Research currents: Writing and the social lives of children. *Language Arts* 62: 632–638.

Graves, Donald H. 1983. *Writing: Teachers and children at work*. Portsmouth, NH: Heinemann.

Temple, Charles, Ruth Nathan, Nancy Burris, and Frances Temple. 1988. *The beginnings of writing*. 2d ed. Boston: Allyn and Bacon.

FOCUS OUTWARD: A WRITING TEACHER TAKES ON THE WORLD

Ruth Nathan

Quite a title, don't you think? Well, if Carl Sagan can describe the origins of intelligence, I reasoned, I can handle the rest of the world, even the feisty young woman destined to sit next to me on my latest flight to Los Angeles:

Her teddy bear flew past my nose so fast I forgot my fear of flying. Then came a plastic bag with mousse and boxed powder, followed by a bunch of fresh flowers, her purse, her headband, and even more, I think

By now, the seat next to me was jam-packed, so I wondered where she'd fit. A few seconds later we were kissin'-cousin close, she with her hands on my arm rests, me sucked in tight to the chair trying to let her by. Eye to eye, with shoes dangling around her neck, red sweatered, and with soft skirt now covering mine and most of me, she took a deep, tired breath and said, "We do what we have to do."

Oh, I loved that line, so I fell in love with her right then. Suddenly the four hours ahead of me seemed fine, just fine.

Then my attention focused on how she'd manage the great sit down, how she'd figure her body in among all that stuff. But even in this strange place she knew her way around. She worked like a teenager who'd been waiting to straighten her clothes-strewn and paper-laden room all week and who'd finally found the time. Her fresh flowers went behind the tray table, the black bag in the pocket below. Her purse flew behind her headrest, and her headband snapped into place. With her teddy between her knees and her shoes balanced over her bulging purse, she tucked in her legs, pushed the hostess button and called for her pillow and blanket, as if for her fiddlers three. We do what we have to do, I thought. Those words will serve her well.

What you've just read is an entry from my *Focus Outward Journal,* a notebook I carry with me in which I enter little paragraphs about things I see. When I don't have my journal, I use loose paper and glue entries in later. I got the idea from Donald Graves about two years ago at a conference in my home state. What a day we had with Graves! He shared his idea: "Just capture the life around you," he said. "Ten minutes a day, just ten minutes a day may change your life."

Oh, how right he was. Since his suggestion, I'll bet I've grown a thousand times over as a writer, a billion times over as a person. Here are a few more entries:

11/15   She was lying with her head back, chin protruding outward, eyes set deep in her head, tapered nose pointing upward waiting for her wash. Clad in gray corduroy jeans, gray loafers, toes turned inward for balance she held a book above her face and read. Her arms must have gotten tired. Slowly, she placed the book on her lap and sat up looking for her colorist. She noticed us and smiled. (In the beauty parlor. Not much for ten minutes. So what!)

11/23   I suppose it might have been the mammoth balloons swaying in the breeze, Betty Boop, Humpty Dumpty, Raggedy Ann, Woody Wood-pecker, that sent my heart beating frantically. Or perhaps it was the roar of the Thanksgiving Day crowd, here in New York, New York, the giant helium bubbles coming close, too close, to the city's telephone poles, mammoth trees, razzle-dazzle, sky-scraping towers. The fear of a big blast? (And what a blast we had!)

Maybe the bands playing Americana did it, with their perfectly synchronized drum majorettes, pulsating pom-poms, swinging silver skirts. Or people watching: the day-glo orange caps, city-slicker strollers, fur coats, multicolored jackets, excited youngsters screaming, Santa, Santa. A Thanksgiving Day parade in New York, squashed between family and friends, roasting chestnuts, hot pretzels dripping with ordinary mustard, balloons of every color, red, yellow, green, blue, turquoise, aqua, char-treuse, purple, crystal. The sunny weather, the gentle breeze, the blue sky painted with ribbons of cotton candy clouds—a great, fun-filled, exhilarating, glad-to-be-alive Thursday in a splashing special, apple-juicy town. (Perhaps a poem someday?)

11/30   Standing on a street corner waiting for the street light to change, I happened to notice a little girl standing next to me. She was holding her grandmother's hand. I saw, from beneath her hat and just above her freckled nose, the longest set of eyelashes I had ever seen. I leaned down and whispered in her ear, "You've got the longest pair of eyelashes I have ever seen." She grinned and her grandma said everyone said that. As the little girl looked upward, her cat-shaped, brilliant green eyes flashed a smackingly rich and youthful innocence that sang of hope, and love, (I'm turning *inward* here, so what . . .) and chocolate, and fairy tales, and stuffed bears, and hearts, and rhymes, and songs, and rocking horses, and dreams, and tinker toys, and cookies with milk, and chocolate chips, and collections, and toy houses with furniture, and trees perfect for climbing, and monopoly, and clubs with friends, and digging to China, and sand castles, and outdoor campfires, and time, lots and lots of time—everything that still means being a little girl to me.

1/21   He sits eating his harmonica, stomping his feet, recklessly strumming that time-worn guitar. Drinking each syllable, hugging each note, John Hammond's got us by the tail! My eyes are so intent, my ears so burning, my mind so engaged that I think I've gone right through him, under his skin and into his heart. It's unbelievable how someone can do this to me.

Do you see what I mean? We can't help but grow capturing stuff like this—and it takes just ten minutes a day.

I'm sharing *Focus Outward* with you for a reason. We've *got* to write if we're going to teach the subject. Nothing in this book makes any sense if we don't perceive ourselves as learners—and I don't know of a living writer today who feels he or she's got it all down pat.

If we don't write, we'll be terrible conference partners—that's the first problem. We'll forget all about the chemical twang, the wildly beating heart, the pain inherent in putting ourselves down on paper and then sharing what we've written with someone else. When I visit classrooms I can always tell if a teacher is truly writing: I just sit in on a teacher-child conference and listen— it's a dead giveaway. Teachers who write know writers need to hear what they've done well first. And writers need to know suggestions come from the heart. Only writers can do this. Only *writers*.

If we write, we know something else: we know how difficult it is to get what we mean down *the way we mean it*. Ideas swirl in our heads, come blasting in at hundreds of miles per hour, but we've got to spill ourselves out slowly. Unlike good comedians, we have no gestures to help us, no intonation cues to guide our listeners. All we've got is a blank sheet of paper and our ability to handle the English language. When we're inexperienced writers, the task is gargantuan; when we're experienced writers, the task is humbling.

In Michigan, the *Focus Outward Journal* has clearly taken off. Not only are teachers keeping them, kids are too. It seems entirely fitting to close this book on writing with *Focus Outward* entries written by children. I'm confident, spelling mistakes and all, that you'll be touched, inspired, perhaps even awed, as I surely am, by what nine- and ten-year-olds see in their experience:

The Wind
Saturday morning when I woke up the wind was blowing hard. Branches had broken off the tree and the rope that was on a branch swinging ten feet in the air because of the wind. The trees were bending at the wind, ice was comming off of the lake from the wind. The dowers [doors] on the house were rateling. The hole house was in havic.

Tom, Grade 5

A Sunday Drive

It was Sunday Apr. 5. A dim Rainy day coming back from basketball. As we drove down twelve mile I noticed a dodge caravan with 3 senior citizens in it. They were all talking at the same time. A long red kite spiraled wildly in the wind like one of Eric Hipple's football passes. As we drove into burger king a graekle looked like he was squaring off to attack us. Then he decided to break-off his challenge when he saw the 2500 lbs. car coming at him. There was a man jogging in a spring coat carring his gloves. "You probably say to yourself whats wrong with that?" It was 25 degrees F outside. A number of Michigan and American flags were flapping in the wind. I suggested to my dad it was for sesquicentinnial. My dad agreed. We wheeled into the drive way. The water of the wet roads splashed against the side of the car.

Matt, Grade 5

The way my mom was prepairing are dinner every body was in her way. Me going in the cookie jar. My brother asking if he could have some ice-cream, then finally My mom just put the knife she was cutting with down and just said "If both of you don't get out the way your going to be grounded." So me and my brother just fule [flew].

Sarah, Grade 5

My Brother

I liked the Day my brother Matt drove his mouth into his donut, the way all the powder and filling of his lemon donut smeared all over his face the way the crumbs, one by one would fall to the car floor the big gulps the way he smacked his lips after each bite, and the sound of um, um, and the way he acted like he never had a donut in his life.

Greg, Grade 5

Inspired? We—Kathy, Frances, Charles, and I—all hope so! Consider "focusing outward" if you feel short on time—because all of us, you too, must write if we're going to teach the subject. Of course the benefits of *Focus Outward* go far beyond the classroom. As Graves said to his waiting audience just two years ago, "It may just change your life." The experience has certainly changed mine. His words have served me well.

Recommended Reading

For Help in Your Classroom

Calkins, Lucy McCormick. *The art of teaching writing.* Portsmouth, NH: Heinemann, 1986.

In this comprehensive book about teaching writing in the elementary school, Calkins tells teachers what to expect from young writers at each grade level. The book contains many practical suggestions with emphasis on establishing a student-oriented attitude for writing in the classroom.

Gentry, J. Richard. *Spel . . . is a four-letter word.* Portsmouth, NH: Heinemann, 1987.

This book presents convincing evidence from case studies and research that encouraging children to write copiously and with invented spelling helps them learn to write and also to spell. Gentry also advocates use of spelling lists beyond grade one.

Gordon, Naomi (ed.). *Classroom experiences: The writing process in action.* Portsmouth, NH: Heinemann, 1984.

K–8 teachers give accounts of the problems, frustrations, and joys in changing from more traditional ways of teaching writing to process writing. One of the most helpful chapters, "Explaining the Writing Process Approach to Parents," contains sample letters from teachers to parents.

Graves, Donald H. *Writing: Teachers and children at work.* Portsmouth, NH: Heinemann, 1983.

Woven throughout this philosophical statement about how writing should be taught, Graves's book contains the author's early ideas about classroom organization, modeling, topic selection, conferencing, and publishing. It was the first process-writing guide for teachers of grades 1–6.

Hansen, Jane, Thomas Newkirk, and Donald Graves (eds.). *Breaking ground: Teachers relate reading and writing in the elementary school.* Portsmouth, NH: Heinemann, 1985.

Thirteen K–8 classroom teachers and seven teacher-educators show how process approaches in writing can be used successfully in the teaching of reading in elementary and middle school.

Kirby, Dan, and Tom Liner. *Inside out: Developmental strategies for teaching writing.* Portsmouth, NH: Boynton/Cook, 1981.

This book has many suggestions for journals and writing across the curriculum. Although it is primarily directed to middle school and high school, most of the activities can be modified for lower grades.

Moffett, James. *Active voice: A writing program across the curriculum.* Portsmouth, NH: Boynton/Cook, 1984.

James Moffet's *Active Voice* sets out a progression of student centered assignments that moves students from personal experience to story to essay according to his own theory of the organization of discourse. The book also describes issues that typically emerge in conferences following each assignment.

Ponsot, Marie, and Rosemary Deen. *Beat not the poor desk: Writing—what to teach, how to teach it, and why.* Portsmouth, NH: Boynton/Cook, 1981.

These authors teach students to handle different kinds of writing by exposing them to models first. While a little far removed from the grade levels about which we've written, their discussion of how good writing serves as models for the students' own writing extends our discussion of modeling and the writing process.

Romano, Tom. *Clearing the way: Working with teenage writers.* Portsmouth, NH: Heinemann, 1987.

Tom Romano, a high-school teacher, gives a rich account of his writing classroom in a voice that sounds committed to his task and to his students. The chapter on evaluation will prove especially helpful to teachers not knowing how to manage a lot of student writing.

Temple, Charles, Ruth Nathan, Nancy Burris, and Frances Temple. *The beginnings of writing.* 2nd ed. Boston: Allyn and Bacon, 1988.

This is in some ways a companion volume to *Classroom Strategies That Work.* The focus is on children's development of concepts about print, spelling, and composing.

Trelease, Jim. *The read-aloud handbook.* 2nd ed. New York: Penguin Books, 1986.

This book contains annotated lists of hundreds of books excellent for reading aloud to children. Its organization by grade level (preschool to eighth grade) within several categories (wordless books, picture books, short novels, novels, poetry) makes it especially convenient to use.

Turbill, Jan. *No better way to teach writing!* Rozelle, NSW, Australia: Primary English Teaching Association, 1982. Distributed in the U.S. by Heinemann, Portsmouth, NH.

———. *Now, we want to write!* Rozelle, NSW, Australia: Primary English Teaching Association, 1983. Distributed in the U.S. by Heinemann, Portsmouth, NH.

No Better Way to Teach Writing! reports on the year-long St. George Project initiating the writing process in twenty-seven elementary classrooms in Australia. It contains many practical suggestions.

Now, We Want to Write!, a sequel to *No Better Way to Teach Writing!*, reports on two more years of the expanded St. George Project.

For Use with a Class

Russell, William F. (ed.) *Classics to read aloud to your children.* New York: Crown Publishers, 1984.

———. *More classics to read aloud to your children.* New York: Crown Publishers, 1986.

These books contain poetry and abridged stories by famous authors—for example, *The Red Badge of Courage* by Stephen Crane, *Call of the Wild* by Jack London, and poems by Longfellow, Kipling, and many more. For each story, the author provides a summary, listening level, approximate reading time, and a pronunciation and vocabulary guide. The books are good sources of material for reading to a class.

Shah, Idries. *World tales: The extraordinary coincidence of stories told in all times, in all places.* New York: Harcourt Brace Jovanovich, 1979. A fantastic source of other cultures' variances of familiar folk tales, this book invites children to spontaneously compare the new tale with the familiar one.

To Help with Your Own Writing

Goldberg, Natalie. *Writing down the bones.* Boston: Shambhala Publications, 1986.

By her personal accounts of experience with writing, the author makes a convincing argument that even the greenest adult writers can succeed with the written word. Goldberg gives many suggestions for experimenting with writing. This book is fun to read and try.

Murray, Donald M. *Write to learn.* New York: Holt, Rinehart and Winston, 1984.

This book is helpful for learning the writing process. The author uses a piece about his grandmother as a step-by-step guide for the reader/writer.

Strunk, William, and E. B. White. *The elements of style.* 3rd ed. New York: Macmillan, 1979.

This slim book on clear writing contains concise information on the rules of language usage. Its format makes it a convenient reference for the writer.

Zinsser, William. *On writing well.* 3rd ed. New York: Harper and Row, 1985.

This book grew out of a course taught by the author at Yale. Its warm style makes easy and pleasant reading. It contains invaluable advice about simple principles and form, including such topics as style, getting rid of clutter, considering audience, writing effective leads and endings, and different types of writing (science, sports, business, humor).

Index